BEGINNING THE WALK ▶

18 SESSIONS ON **JESUS**

THE WAY

THE TRUTH

& THE LIFE

A NavPress resource published in alliance
with Tyndale House Publishers, Inc.

NavPress is the publishing ministry of The Navigators, an international Christian organization and leader in personal spiritual development. NavPress is committed to helping people grow spiritually and enjoy lives of meaning and hope through personal and group resources that are biblically rooted, culturally relevant, and highly practical.

For more information, visit www.NavPress.com.

Beginning the Walk: 18 Sessions on Jesus the Way, the Truth, and the Life

Collected edition copyright © 2018 by Navigator Church Ministries. All rights reserved.

Individual titles (*Jesus the Way, Jesus the Truth, Jesus the Life*) copyright © 2004 by Navigator Church Ministries.

A NavPress resource published in alliance with Tyndale House Publishers, Inc.

NAVPRESS and the NAVPRESS logo are registered trademarks of NavPress, The Navigators, Colorado Springs, CO. *TYNDALE* is a registered trademark of Tyndale House Publishers, Inc. *NCM* and the NCM logo are trademarks of The Navigators, Colorado Springs, CO. Absence of ® in connection with marks of NavPress or other parties does not indicate an absence of registration of those marks.

The Team:
Don Pape, Publisher
David Zimmerman, Editor
Helen Macdonald, Copyeditor
Jennifer Ghionzoli, Designer

Cover photograph of mountain hike copyright © by Galen Crout/Unsplash.com. All rights reserved.

Bridge to Life by The Navigators copyright © 1969. Used by permission of The Navigators. All rights reserved.

Cover title Cache font copyright © by Quill Type Co/Creative Market. All rights reserved.

Some of the anecdotal illustrations in this book are true to life and are included with the permission of the persons involved. All other illustrations are composites of real situations, and any resemblance to people living or dead is purely coincidental.

For information about special discounts for bulk purchases, please contact Tyndale House Publishers at csresponse@tyndale.com, or call 1-800-323-9400.

ISBN 978-1-63146-924-4

Printed in the United States of America

23 22 21 20 19 18
 6   5   4   3   2   1

CONTENTS

PREFACE

Therefore as you have received Christ Jesus the Lord,
so walk in Him.

COLOSSIANS 2:6, NASB

WELCOME TO AN INCREDIBLE JOURNEY called "your new life in Christ." When you came to a personal faith in Christ, you began a lifelong journey that you will complete only when you see Jesus face-to-face. He made this claim and promise in John 10:10: "I came so they can have real and eternal life, more and better life than they ever dreamed of."

Whenever the Bible talks about new life (or as *The Message* puts it, "more and better life"), it is talking about more than just new habits or patterns for daily living. The life that results from faith in Christ is life with a new spiritual dimension. It is a relational journey that has adventure, excitement, and purpose. The Bible uses the term "eternal life" to describe this new reality. Jesus explained it like this in John 17:3: "This is the real and eternal life: that they know you, the one and only true God, and Jesus Christ, whom you sent."

Life, in the language of the Bible, is not a single event. It is a journey of knowing Christ, experiencing the reality of His presence in your life, and discovering more of who He is as you walk through each day. This life has both quality and quantity. In terms of quality, God gives meaning and purpose to the practical experiences of life. In terms of quantity, this relationship with Christ lasts from the moment of your faith discovery until . . . forever.

Jesus Christ is the central focus of this life. As you become more familiar with the Bible, you will discover how important Jesus really is. Most of us have developed a working concept of God based on our past experiences. For some, God is a distant landlord; to others, He is a vigilant policeman. Still others see God as an impersonal force or a cosmic Santa Claus. Jesus Christ came into our world to reveal the true nature and person of God. He came to correct and clarify our understanding of God. To know Christ is to discover God, as we see in Hebrews 1:1-3:

> Going through a long line of prophets, God has been addressing our ancestors in different ways for centuries. Recently he spoke to us directly through his Son. By his Son, God created the world in the beginning, and it will all belong to the Son at the end. This Son perfectly mirrors God, and is stamped with God's nature. He holds everything together by what he says—powerful words!

The journey of knowing Christ is more than gathering information, yet it needs to be grounded in truth. This journey is more than an emotional event, yet it contains many significant experiences. This relational journey touches every part of who we are. It affects our minds, emotions, and wills. It works from the inside out and the outside in. It is personal. It is private and public. It is visible and invisible, simple and complex. It is incomprehensible yet understandable. It is beyond our experience yet touches everything about us that is real.

God is the designer and author of life, so understanding who He is will help you appreciate the gift of life He has given you. *Beginning the Walk* will move you along on your journey of knowing and experiencing Christ personally.

As you begin your journey, you may wish you had maps or blueprints to show you where to go or what to do. This study can help. Some of the concepts introduced in these pages may be totally new for you, and some may be familiar. Some may challenge what you previously thought, and others may even be confusing. Remember that this is a lifelong journey—a journey that will take you into new discoveries and experiences. Clarity will come as you continue on the journey.

The Bible is our primary source for truth on this journey. Written over the course of fifteen hundred years by various authors who were inspired by God, the Bible includes a number of literary styles. Some of it is written as history, some as poetry. Some of the books are letters to individuals; others are letters to groups of people. The Bible claims to be the revelation of God to man, God's own story line with man. By studying the Bible, we can move beyond the general revelation of God that we see in nature to discover His character, heart, and purposes.

In the past, you may have found the Bible boring, baffling, or bewildering. Now, however, as you begin your relational journey with Christ, the Bible will come alive. As you read the Bible, you will begin to understand what it means to have a new life in Christ.

The Bible will be your best resource for the journey. But as with any journey, there will be times when you feel lost or unsure about which path to take. That's because a life of faith prompts just as many questions as answers.

A few years ago, an airline company offered mystery trips. People bought tickets and showed up at the airport with bags packed for a three-day journey. All arrangements were made for a surprise weekend in a major city in the United States, but ticket holders wouldn't know which one until they got on the plane. The mystery added a sense of adventure to an otherwise familiar activity.

But what if, instead of US cities, the plane whisked you off to a mystery location unlike anything you had ever known? One where *everything* seemed new and unfamiliar. One where the culture, the government, the language, the currency, even the landscape were foreign.

When you came to personal faith in Jesus Christ, you were given a ticket for this kind of mystery trip. And now that the plane has landed, you have stepped into a place called the Kingdom of God. While you will probably have lots of questions about this place, you will soon discover that the Kingdom of God promises real-life adventure in the "now" as well as an incomprehensibly exciting "not yet" called heaven. You will learn that living in the Kingdom of God brings new freedoms and new relationships; that it results in a new perspective, purpose, and direction; and that it gives you new resources and responsibilities.

Teaching you how to relate to Jesus Christ and to live successfully in the "now" aspect of the Kingdom is the purpose of *Beginning the Walk*. Regardless of your religious (or nonreligious) background, these lessons will help you understand more about the exciting journey you began by putting your faith in Christ.

The apostle Paul said that new life in Christ brings about significant changes. In 2 Corinthians 5:17, he wrote to the new believers in Corinth, "Therefore if anyone is in Christ, he is a new creature; the old things passed away; behold, new things have come" (NASB). As you begin to understand these changes, you will be better able to participate in your new life adventure. You will be able to fully utilize the resources and enjoy all the benefits of life in the Kingdom of God.

Enjoy the journey!

HOW TO USE
BEGINNING THE WALK

BEGINNING THE WALK is designed to help a person begin a new life with Christ. You can work through this material on your own, with a mentor, or in a small group. You don't need an extensive church or religious background to get started. Each lesson will help you understand an important element of a lifelong relationship with Christ.

Beginning the Walk is divided into three sections:

- Jesus the Way
- Jesus the Truth
- Jesus the Life

Each section contains six lessons, each of which begins with a summary statement and a key Scripture. These provide a quick overview of the lesson content. As you work through the lesson, read through each subheading and underline ideas that stand out to you or concepts that create questions. If you are doing the study with others, stop at the end of each topic and discuss what you have read to gain clarity. If you are working through the material on your own, find a trusted mentor with whom you can explore your questions. Most sections have questions for reflection and understanding. Taking time to answer them will help you grasp what you are reading.

At the end of each lesson you will find a summary statement that pulls together the key ideas of the lesson. Be sure to read those as a way of clarifying what is important to remember. The last part of each lesson is a prayer. It is best to read this prayer out loud. This will help you respond to God in prayer regarding what He has been saying to you through His Word. This pattern forms a conversational dialogue that is at the heart of this new relationship.

The majority of the Bible passages used in *Beginning the Walk* are included in the text of the lessons. Still, we recommend you have a personal Bible as well. In addition to reading the Scripture in the lesson, you may want to look up the references and read them in your own Bible (see appendix 3 for guidance on Bible reading). This will broaden your understanding as you discover more about the context of the Scripture passages.

Each lesson is designed to help you understand your new spiritual journey. Living your new life in Christ may at times seem at odds with what you have thought in the past. To help you review and remember the important concepts, you will find a summary page at the end of each of the three major sections. These are designed to give you a clear and quick overview of all that you have studied.

At the back of the book you will find three appendixes. The first offers an explanation of how to establish a faith-based relationship with Christ. If you are not sure that you have ever received God's gift of forgiveness and been accepted into His family of faith, this explanation will show you how. It can also serve as a way to explain to others how you have received new life in Christ.

The second appendix offers an extensive set of passages from the Bible that will help you remember what is true about you because of your relationship with God in Christ. These verses can be particularly helpful to counter other voices that might lie to you about who you are in Christ.

The third appendix gives you several ways to continue your walk with Christ beyond this study. It explains how to effectively read the Bible and memorize key verses. These spiritual practices are essential for building a lifelong pursuit of following Christ.

JESUS THE WAY

For there is hope to attain a journey's end when there is a path which stretches between the traveller and his goal. But if there is no path, or if a man does not know which way to go, there is little use in knowing the destination. As it is, there is one road, and one only, well secured against all possibility of going astray; and this road is provided by one who is himself both God and man. As God, he is the goal; as man, he is the way.

SAINT AUGUSTINE, *CITY OF GOD*

YOU MAY HAVE COME TO FAITH in Jesus Christ at a very identifiable moment in your life or through a process that is less definable. You may have endured significant crises that propelled you along in your search for God, or your story may be one of a quiet heart tug. Regardless of the path you took to Christ, those steps are only the beginning. Faith in Christ launches a relational journey with Christ in His Kingdom. This journey has a beginning but no end. It is the kind of life that is eternal.

Christianity was initially called "the Way." Followers of Christ were identified with a way of life Jesus demonstrated and taught. Jesus even referred to Himself as "the way" in John 14:6: "I am the way, and the truth, and the life" (NASB).

Walking with Jesus Christ on this journey will bring both internal and external changes. Some changes will happen quickly, while others will take years. The apostle Paul referred to things being "new" for those in Christ. As we journey on with Christ, our behavior changes, our thinking changes, even our desires and values change. Life really does become new.

For any journey to be successful, you have to first prepare. This includes knowing where you are going and how you are going to get there. To help you prepare for your faith journey, this study will introduce basic concepts that can help you avoid painful detours and roadblocks.

These concepts are themes taught throughout the Bible. We have chosen to focus primarily on two books in the New Testament: Ephesians and Colossians, two letters written by the apostle Paul during his ministry in the first century. They were written to groups of new believers in Christ who were beginning their own journeys.

These are the concepts you'll explore in "Jesus the Way":

- Your New Connection in Christ
- Your New Creation in Christ
- Your New Center in Christ
- Your New Companionship in Christ
- Your New Clothes in Christ
- Your New Calling in Christ

LESSON 1

NEW CONNECTION

Your journey with Christ involves a new relationship with God: a personal connection. Faith in Christ breaks down the barrier separating us from God and gives us access to a deep, personal friendship with the eternal God.

Now God has us where he wants us, with all the time in this world and the next to shower grace and kindness upon us in Christ Jesus.

EPHESIANS 2:7

WHILE IN THE ARMY'S Infantry Officer Candidate School, I (Ron) was part of a military honor guard that welcomed the president of the United States to our military base. He walked so close to me that I could have reached out and touched him. For a brief moment I caught his eye. That is a far cry from having a personal friendship with the president, but it's the closest I've been to a powerful leader. It seems as if the more powerful a leader is, the more distant and unapproachable he or she becomes to ordinary people.

What a contrast this is to the approachability of Jesus! The awesome creator of the universe planned long ago to relate to each person "up close and personal." Jesus' role in history made that possible. Regardless of your past, God wants a personal relationship with you.

There are two key aspects of any relationship: honest dialogue and shared experiences. Both are essential. Dialogue without mutual experiences leaves you intellectually stimulated but relationally challenged. Shared experiences can be enjoyable, but without dialogue they remain shallow and incomplete. Relating to Christ works in much the same way. He wants both your dialogue and your experiences.

So who is this God who wants a relationship with you? The Bible begins with the words "In the beginning God . . ." (Genesis 1:1, NASB). The Bible doesn't set out to prove God but rather reveals Him. In the Old Testament, God is described as "powerful," "holy," and "mighty."[1] Unlike most other religions, the God of the Bible is not just the supreme God; He is the one and only God.

The Bible also shows God as having three personalities or distinct persons. This concept is called the Trinity or Tri-unity. Easton's *Illustrated Bible Dictionary* says,

> *Trinity*, a word not found in Scripture, but used to express the doctrine of the unity of God as subsisting in three distinct Persons. . . .
>
> The propositions involved in the doctrine are these: 1. That God is one, and that there is but one God. . . . 2. That the Father is a distinct divine Person . . . distinct from the Son and the Holy Spirit. 3. That Jesus Christ was truly God, and yet was a Person distinct from the Father and the Holy Spirit. 4. That the Holy Spirit is also a distinct divine Person.[2]

When people relate to God, they relate both to God as "one" and to God as expressed in each person of the Trinity. This becomes more evident in the New Testament, where the persons of the Trinity are referred to more directly in their unique roles. Jesus is often referred to as the second person of the Trinity, God the Son, and is the focal point of the Gospels, the first four books of the New Testament. The Holy Spirit, referred to as the third person of the Trinity, is the focal point of the book of Acts. When the apostle Paul and the other writers wrote to the early churches, they used the term *God*, referring to the first person of the Trinity, or God the Father.

Let's look at how each person of the Trinity is involved in the new connection you have with God.

LOVED BY THE FATHER

In stark contrast to the pagan gods or the sketches of God as expressed in various other religions, our God is revealed not only as powerful and holy but as intimately loving. The apostle Paul described God in Ephesians 1:3-6:

> How blessed is God! And what a blessing he is! He's the Father of our Master, Jesus Christ, and takes us to the high places of blessing in him. Long before he laid down earth's foundations, he had us in mind, had settled on us as the focus of his love, to be made whole and holy by his love. Long, long ago he decided to adopt us into his family through Jesus Christ. (What pleasure he took in planning this!) He wanted us to enter into the celebration of his lavish gift-giving by the hand of his beloved Son.

Q1. What do you discover about God from these verses?

Q2. What does it mean to you when someone or something is the "focus" of love?

Q3. **Which of these statements have you believed? Why?**

_____ I am too insignificant to be important to God.

_____ I have too much baggage in my life to ever receive God's love.

_____ I don't deserve God's love, so I can't accept it.

_____ God is too distant for someone to relate to on a personal level.

Q4. **What does this passage say about your value to God?**

One way the apostle Paul described your new relationship with God was by the term _adoption_. In Paul's culture, people adopted children when they had no legal heir. A child who was adopted gained a permanent legal name and all the privileges of a biological son or daughter—most notably, an inheritance.

The apostle John referred to the same idea in John 1:12: "Yet to all who received him [Jesus Christ], to those who believed in his name, he gave the right to become children of God" (NIV).

FREED BY THE SON

Freedom, in part, comes as you are released from your past guilt and separation from God and brought into a personal and vital relationship with Christ. A fish tossed onto the banks of a river is initially very active but not free. Placed back into the water, the fish is truly free. Living without faith in God is like being a fish on the bank. You may be frantically active, but you are doomed. Freedom comes as you are placed into the environment you were designed for, the safe and secure love of God.

To experience your freedom, you must understand two foundational truths regarding your new connection. One is that you are "in Christ," and the second is that Christ is "in you." They are like opposite sides of the same coin, linked together to form the whole. Part of the miracle of experiencing Christ is that both of these truths became a reality the moment you came to faith in Christ. However, it is a lifelong journey to understand and work out the implications of these two truths.

Being "in Christ" means that you now share His identity. It means that God sees you just as He sees Jesus. As Jesus is God's Son, you are also now one of His children. Because Jesus is accepted before God, you also are accepted, with your sins forgiven.

Christ "in you" means that Christ makes your heart His dwelling place. In the Old Testament, God's presence was in the Hebrew Tabernacle (or Temple) in a place called the Holy of Holies. Since the death and resurrection of Jesus Christ, God now lives in the hearts of His people. The apostle Paul explained it as follows in Ephesians 1:7-12:

> Because of the sacrifice of the Messiah, his blood poured out on the altar of the Cross, we're a free people—free of penalties and punishments chalked up by all our misdeeds. And not just barely free, either. *Abundantly* free! He thought of everything, provided for everything we could possibly need, letting us in on the plans he took such delight in making. He set it all out before us in Christ, a long-range plan in which everything would be brought together and summed up in him, everything in deepest heaven, everything on planet earth.
>
> It's in Christ that we find out who we are and what we are living for. Long before we first heard of Christ and got our hopes up, he had his eye on us, had designs on us for glorious living, part of the overall purpose he is working out in everything and everyone.

Q5. As described in the preceding passage, what was accomplished by Christ's sacrifice for you on the cross?

Misdeeds (or *sins*) means missing the mark of God's moral standard. It refers to both the inward state of your heart and your outward behavior.

Q6. Look again at Ephesians 1:7-12. What are the benefits of being "in Christ"?

Both your identity and your destiny are wrapped up in your relationship with Christ. Discovering who Christ is and what He is doing is key to knowing how you should live. He desires to bring you alongside Him and make your life work. Jesus said in Matthew 11:28-30,

> Are you tired? Worn out? Burned out on religion? Come to me. Get away with me and you'll recover your life. I'll show you how to take a real rest. Walk with me and work with me—watch how I do it. Learn the unforced rhythms of grace. I won't lay anything heavy or ill-fitting on you. Keep company with me and you'll learn to live freely and lightly.

CERTIFIED BY THE HOLY SPIRIT

The role of the Holy Spirit, the third person of the Trinity, took on a new significance after Christ was crucified, rose again, and ascended into heaven. Jesus told His disciples to get ready because things were going to be different. No longer was God simply going to be present alongside them, but He was actually going to live *in* each person of faith. The Holy

Spirit is also God's seal of certification in your life that you are officially His. The apostle Paul said the following in Ephesians 1:13-14:

> It's in Christ that you, once you heard the truth and believed it (this Message of your salvation), found yourselves home free—signed, sealed, and delivered by the Holy Spirit. This signet from God is the first installment on what's coming, a reminder that we'll get everything God has planned for us, a praising and glorious life.

God has not only forgiven you; He actually lives in you. The Holy Spirit's presence in your life is a seal (signet) of that truth. Just as a king's seal was the official stamp of authenticity, the Holy Spirit is your seal giving authenticity to your new connection with God. This may not seem real to you now, but it is true nonetheless. You will learn as you walk with Christ how to recognize the reality of God's Spirit within you.

Q7. What did you learn about the Holy Spirit from this passage in Ephesians?

One of the things the Holy Spirit does is help you understand who God is and who you are. He works quietly in your inner person to bring clarity and awareness. The apostle Paul described it as follows in Romans 8:16: "God's Spirit touches our spirits and confirms who we really are. We know who he is, and we know who we are: Father and children."

The Holy Spirit's presence also serves as a reminder that there is more to come. God has an inheritance for you that is a future reality. We can apply to ourselves what Jesus reminded the disciples just before He was to leave them to take His place in heaven:

> Don't let this throw you. You trust God, don't you? Trust me. There is plenty of room for you in my Father's home. If that weren't so,

would I have told you that I'm on my way to get a room ready for you? And if I'm on my way to get your room ready, I'll come back and get you so you can live where I live.

JOHN 14:1-3

Q8. What do these verses promise you as a member of God's family?

SUMMARY

Through faith we have a new relationship with God that is reflected in each person of the Trinity: Father, Son, and Holy Spirit. Our journey is based on a personal, dynamic relationship with God as expressed in each person of the Trinity:

- Loved by the Father
- Freed by the Son
- Certified by the Holy Spirit

PRAYER

Thank You, God, for making it possible for me to relate to You personally. I realize that I have no merit of my own that would earn me the right to come into Your presence. As Your adopted child, I want to know You more and learn how to live as a member of Your family. Open my mind and change my heart so I would know the joy of a deep friendship with You.

NEW CREATION

Your journey with Christ begins with God giving you a new nature.
We are new creations. We may look the same on the outside, but something
inside has changed dramatically. We are now in Christ, and Christ is in us.
This results in a new identity.

*Now we look inside, and what we see is that anyone united with
the Messiah gets a fresh start, is created new. The old life is gone;
a new life burgeons! Look at it!*

2 CORINTHIANS 5:17

EARLY IN THE COLD WAR, a Russian pilot flew his MiG fighter plane
to Japan and asked for asylum in the United States. After the predict-
able flurry of excitement over having a state-of-the-art Russian plane to
analyze, government officials debriefed the pilot and eventually brought
him to the United States,[1] where he was given a new identity and citizenship. He was instructed in the beliefs and systems of his new country and
given financial resources to get started in his new life.

Interviewed years later, the pilot reflected on how difficult it initially
was living with his new identity. He had been told he was free, yet he
imagined the KGB or the US equivalent was shadowing his every move.
He had the freedom to travel anywhere he wanted but still felt as if he
needed to ask permission. At times he experienced an unexplainable urge
to go back to the life he had willingly left—to go back to the "known"—
even though that meant certain death.

You are probably experiencing similar adjustment challenges. It takes time for your perspective, values, and behavior to change, yet faith in Christ instantly changes your standing with God. Your position with God is not based on how you feel or even act. It is based on what Christ has done for you at the Cross. Too often new believers base their standing with God on how they feel at a given moment or on their behavior. Don't make this mistake. Base your standing with God on what He has said is true about you.

YOU ARE ALIVE

The Bible describes our life outside of a relationship with Christ as being "dead." We are cut off or separated from a vital and personal connection with God and His Spirit. But when we accept Christ by faith, we are made "alive." The apostle Paul wrote in Ephesians 2:1-6,

> It wasn't so long ago that you were mired in that old stagnant life of sin. You let the world, which doesn't know the first thing about living, tell you how to live. You filled your lungs with polluted unbelief, and then exhaled disobedience. We all did it, all of us doing what we felt like doing, when we felt like doing it, all of us in the same boat. It's a wonder God didn't lose his temper and do away with the whole lot of us. Instead, immense in mercy and with an incredible love, he embraced us. He took our sin-dead lives and made us alive in Christ. He did all this on his own, with no help from us! Then he picked us up and set us down in highest heaven in company with Jesus, our Messiah.

Q1.   How did Paul describe life before coming to faith in Christ?

Q2. What did God do for you?

Q3. Why did He do it?

Becoming alive implies that we were previously dead. In Genesis 3, we read the story of how, through Adam and Eve, humanity became spiritually dead. You may not have thought of yourself as dead, but that is how God describes a person without Christ. This concept is repeated throughout Scripture. It graphically illustrates the sorry state of life without God and the dramatic change that takes place when one comes to Christ by faith. Being dead like this explains a lot about your past. Being made alive implies a lot about your future.

This new aliveness may manifest itself in various ways in your life. Some notice it as an appetite for the Bible, the Word of God. Others discover it in the peace they find or in their freedom from guilt. It may start as a seed of awareness and grow. Regardless of how you feel, God has given you new life. Believe it and watch how it displays itself day by day.

YOU ARE A SAINT

The apostle Paul began most of his letters to the early churches with the greeting "To the saints."[2] Saints! When you read the letters and learn about some of the issues and problems those new believers were having, you might question Paul's greeting. The word *saint* fundamentally signifies someone who is separated, sanctified, or holy.[3]

God's declaration of our holiness is not a response to our perfection. God calls us holy because He no longer sees us on the basis of our own merit (how good or how sinful we are) but through the perfection of His Son. You are no longer referred to as a sinner who is separate from God but as a saint who still sins. God has established your core identity as that of a saint. Your journey involves learning how to live as a saint or a "set-apart one." The apostle Paul said it this way in Colossians 1:21-22:

> You yourselves are a case study of what he does. At one time you all had your backs turned to God, thinking rebellious thoughts of him, giving him trouble every chance you got. But now, by giving himself completely at the Cross, actually *dying* for you, Christ brought you over to God's side and put your lives together, whole and holy in his presence.

Q4. In the previous passage, circle the things that are true about you now.

Q5. What do you think it means to be "brought over to God's side"?

YOU ARE FORGIVEN

Another part of your new identity is that you are forgiven. God did not ignore your sin but in fact dealt with it through Jesus' sacrifice on the cross. Forgiveness was not free. Christ did what we could not do on our own.

Throughout the Old Testament as God related to the nation of Israel, He established an elaborate system of sacrifices that dealt with the issue of sin. Much of the symbolism of that system is lost in our culture, but there is no doubt that God takes sin seriously. Sin offends His very nature. The beauty of Jesus' sacrifice is that through it, God's character is revealed in wonderful fullness—including both His love and His justice. The apostle Paul said in Colossians 2:13-14,

When you were stuck in your old sin-dead life, you were incapable of responding to God. God brought you alive—right along with Christ! Think of it! All sins forgiven, the slate wiped clean, that old arrest warrant canceled and nailed to Christ's cross.

Q6. What do these verses say God has done for you in Christ?

Q7. Because these things are true, how should you respond?

YOU ARE A CITIZEN

The apostle Paul talked about this new journey of faith as life in a new country or kingdom. This word picture helps us see who we are in light of both Christ (the King of the Kingdom) and our fellow travelers. During His ministry, Christ talked a great deal about the Kingdom of God. The concept of a kingdom isn't particularly relevant in modern society. We have to look back to medieval times or perhaps to the images in Tolkien's *The Lord of the Rings* to find a kingdom reference point. Yet the Kingdom of God is not a geographic place with castles, kings, or moats. Paul referred to it as the household of faith. It is a personal reality that deals with the hearts and souls of women and men.

In Ephesians 2:19, the apostle Paul wrote as follows:

That's plain enough, isn't it? You're no longer wandering exiles. This kingdom of faith is now your home country. You're no longer strangers or outsiders. You *belong* here, with as much right to the name Christian as anyone. God is building a home. He's using us all—irrespective of how we got here—in what he is building.

And again in Colossians 1:13-14:

> God rescued us from dead-end alleys and dark dungeons. He's set
> us up in the kingdom of the Son he loves so much, the Son who got
> us out of the pit we were in, got rid of the sins we were doomed to
> keep repeating.

Q8.   What do these verses tell you about being a citizen of God's Kingdom?

YOU ARE FAMILY

Paul also described those who follow Christ as being "insiders" or family members. As a family member, you are a member of a new community of brothers and sisters. No longer are you identified based on your physical, ethnic, or religious identity. No matter what you were before, you are now part of a family with rights to all its privileges and responsibilities.

Every culture has its criteria for becoming an "insider." It could be based on looks, language, or city of origin. In Paul's culture, there were two main divisions. The religious Jews were the insiders; the pagan Gentiles, the outsiders. But when Jesus arrived on the scene, He changed the picture. No longer were the Jews the only people who had an "in" with God.

The apostle Paul said in Ephesians 2:11-13,

> But don't take any of this for granted. It was only yesterday that
> you outsiders to God's ways had no idea of any of this, didn't know
> the first thing about the way God works, hadn't the faintest idea
> of Christ. You knew nothing of that rich history of God's covenants
> and promises in Israel, hadn't a clue about what God was doing

in the world at large. Now because of Christ—dying that death, shedding that blood—you who were once out of it altogether are in on everything.

And again in Colossians 1:26-27:

This mystery has been kept in the dark for a long time, but now it's out in the open. God wanted everyone, not just Jews, to know this rich and glorious secret inside and out, regardless of their background, regardless of their religious standing. The mystery in a nutshell is just this: Christ is in you, so therefore you can look forward to sharing in God's glory. It's that simple. That is the substance of our Message.

Q9. What do these passages say about you as a member of God's family?

On a news program, a reporter revealed that millions of dollars of inheritance are locked up in the vaults of city and state governments. Jewelry, stocks, and cash, each clearly identified with the names of the inheritors, remain unclaimed. The reason the treasures remain unclaimed is that the inheritors are unaware of their existence.

The treasure is there, taking up space in a vault and waiting to be claimed. All it takes is for the right people to identify themselves and collect what is legally theirs. As a child of God, you also have an inheritance waiting for you. Paul prayed the following prayer for the new believers in Ephesus:

I pray that the eyes of your heart may be enlightened, so that you will know what is the hope of His calling, what are the riches of the glory of His inheritance in the saints, and what is the surpassing greatness of His power toward us who believe. These are in accordance with the working of the strength of His might.

EPHESIANS 1:18-19, NASB

Living in light of your inheritance is part of the joy of discovery along the journey. Paul wrote in Ephesians 1:3-8,

How blessed is God! And what a blessing he is! He's the Father of our Master, Jesus Christ, and takes us to the high places of blessing in him. Long before he laid down earth's foundations, he had us in mind, had settled on us as the focus of his love, to be made whole and holy by his love. Long, long ago he decided to adopt us into his family through Jesus Christ. (What pleasure he took in planning this!) He wanted us to enter into the celebration of his lavish gift-giving by the hand of his beloved Son. Because of the sacrifice of the Messiah, his blood poured out on the altar of the Cross, we're a free people—free of penalties and punishments chalked up by all our misdeeds. And not just barely free, either. *Abundantly* free! He thought of everything, provided for everything we could possibly need.

Q10. According to the previous passage, what is your inheritance as a family member?

Q11. What might be the consequences of not knowing about or not claiming your inheritance?

SUMMARY

In Christ you are a brand-new creation. God has changed your essential being. He has not only forgiven you but has also given you a brand-new identity. You are now spiritually alive, a saint, a citizen of God's Kingdom, and a rightful member of His family.

PRAYER

Father, I admit that I don't always feel like the person You say I am. I need Your help in changing the way I think about You and myself. It is awesome that You have made me Your child and given me the rights and privileges of a family member. Help me live today in light of my new identity and experience more of its reality in my heart and mind.

NEW CENTER

Your journey with Christ takes you into brand-new territory.
In order to understand where you are going, it's important to see the big picture.
Christ is at the center, and He is the source of everything you will need.
Because of His centrality you will have a new perspective on all you do and say.

We look at this Son and see the God who cannot be seen.
We look at this Son and see God's original purpose in everything created.
COLOSSIANS 1:15

PAUL, WRITING TO A GROUP of first-century new believers in the Roman city of Colossae, described the centrality of Christ in the world and in the life of each believer:

> We look at this Son and see the God who cannot be seen. We look at this Son and see God's original purpose in everything created. For everything, absolutely everything, above and below, visible and invisible, rank after rank after rank of angels—*everything* got started in him and finds its purpose in him. He was there before any of it came into existence and holds it all together right up to this moment. And when it comes to the church, he organizes and holds it together, like a head does a body. He was supreme in the beginning and—leading the resurrection parade—he is supreme

in the end. From beginning to end he's there, towering far above everything, everyone.

COLOSSIANS 1:15-18

Q1. What does this passage tell you about Jesus?

Q2. What is your initial reaction to what Paul said about Jesus? How does what Paul said influence what you think about Jesus?

The term *church* originally referred to an assembly or popular meeting, especially a religious congregation. The word *church* can also refer to believers in Christ no matter where they are; it is not limited by geography. The "body of Christ" metaphor Paul mentioned in the Colossians passage above paints a picture of the church that suggests the way the church works (or ought to work).

Today we often use the term *church* to describe a building where Christians go to worship. Yet when the Bible talks about a church, it is referring not to a steeple-topped building but to a group of believers meeting together. There were no church buildings in New Testament times, so believers met in private homes.

Q3. How do these statements regarding the church compare to what you have believed in the past?

CHRIST THE REVEALER OF GOD

The Rosetta Stone is a compact igneous slab that was found in 1799 in the small Egyptian village of Rosetta. It contains three inscriptions that represent a single text. Its discovery signaled a breakthrough in the research of Egyptian hieroglyphs. The representation of a single text in the three script variants enabled the French scholar Jean-François Champollion in 1822 to decipher hieroglyphs, which up to that time were not understood.

Jesus is God's Rosetta Stone. God, only partially understood from reading the Old Testament, is revealed through Jesus in language we understand. He is God in human form, living among us.

Jesus is the revelation of God. By looking at Jesus, we can see God. The Old Testament is not merely a collection of history books, but a revelation of who God is. In the Old Testament, God revealed Himself as He related to specific people and groups of people over hundreds of years. Through reading their stories, we learn something of the nature of God. But the greatest revelation of God came when He entered our space-time world as one of us. Jesus, also called the Christ or Messiah, is God in human form, revealing a true picture of God.

Jesus, or Jesus of Nazareth, was the common name given to God the Son when He came into human form. Jesus was also given various explanatory titles during His life and ministry. He was called Teacher, Master, or Lord. He claimed to be the Son of God (or Son) and the Jewish Messiah, the promised deliverer of Israel. The term *Christ* is the Greek translation of the Jewish title *Messiah*. Jesus is often referred to in the Bible as Christ or Jesus the Christ. Today we refer to Him as Jesus Christ, often incorrectly assuming it is a first and last name. Actually, it is a first name and a title.

The New Testament book of Hebrews was written to help us understand more of who Jesus is and how He clarifies the events and messages of the Old Testament. Hebrews 1:1-4 (NIV) speaks of Jesus as the Son of God:

In the past God spoke to our ancestors through the prophets at
many times and in various ways, but in these last days he has

spoken to us by his Son, whom he appointed heir of all things, and through whom he made the universe. The Son is the radiance of God's glory and the exact representation of his being, sustaining all things by his powerful word. After he had provided purification for sins, he sat down at the right hand of the Majesty in heaven. So he became as much superior to the angels as the name he has inherited is superior to theirs.

Q4. What does this passage tell you about Jesus?

In essence, the writer of Hebrews was saying, "If you want to know what God is like, look at Jesus." Jesus made the same connection when Philip, one of His disciples, asked Jesus to show him the Father (God):

Philip said, "Master, show us the Father; then we'll be content." [Jesus replied,] "You've been with me all this time, Philip, and you still don't understand? To see me is to see the Father. So how can you ask, 'Where is the Father?'"
JOHN 14:8-9

The Bible tells us that in order to understand and know God, we must concentrate on knowing and understanding Jesus. The first four books of the New Testament, referred to as the Gospels, are unique accounts of the life and ministry of Jesus. The rest of the New Testament is made up primarily of letters about Jesus written by apostles to first-century believers. Today we not only have the Bible that gives us the historical view, but we also have the Holy Spirit who gives us understanding.

In our culture, people tend to treat the invisible as less real than the visible. Yet with a little reflection, we must admit that much of what is real in our world is invisible. Jesus, no longer physically present, is still present through His Spirit. Jesus told His initial disciples that after His resurrection, His presence would be even greater. His physical presence limited Jesus to a single location at a given time. But after His resurrection, through His Spirit, He is now universally present in all believers, all the time, everywhere.

Q5. How can a person know and relate to Jesus, who is present yet invisible?

Communication with Jesus is possible today. As you read the Bible, God can speak to you. The Bible can show you how to live effectively. It is a personal love letter written by God to each of His children.

You can also communicate with Jesus through prayer. Prayer doesn't require big, fancy words or a specific location or posture. Prayer is simply talking to God by telling Him what you know about Him, expressing your concerns and asking for His help, and thanking Him for His answers.

Take time each day this week to read the Bible and pray. Express to God what you are learning. Through this spiritual dialogue, you will grow a powerful and real relationship with God.

CHRIST THE LEADER

The Bible teaches that although Christ came quietly into our world as a baby, lived as an obscure teacher in an out-of-the-way nation, died a criminal's cruel death, and was buried in a borrowed grave, He is anything but insignificant.

The Romans considered the title given to Jesus, "King of the Jews," and saw no threat to their control. To them He was a minor irritation, easily dealt with and summarily dismissed. What they failed to see was that this ordinary-looking man would build a mighty Kingdom that would outlast Rome and every other nation in history. His Kingdom would start small, grow until it eclipsed them all, and then, amazingly, last forever.

The Old Testament paints two pictures of the coming Messiah, of Jesus. In one picture, Jesus is painted as a king. In the other, He is painted as a servant. The first-century Jews fully expected their Messiah to come into the world as a king—to take charge, rid them of the oppressive rule of Rome, and set them politically free. Jesus of Nazareth was a disappointment to them. He led no revolution against Roman rule but instead taught about God and a Kingdom that seemed strangely vague.

Paul wrote the following in Ephesians 1:20-22:

> All this energy issues from Christ: God raised him from death
> and set him on a throne in deep heaven, in charge of running
> the universe, everything from galaxies to governments,
> no name and no power exempt from his rule. And not just for
> the time being, but *forever*. He is in charge of it all, has the final
> word on everything.

Q6. What does this passage say is true about Jesus?

Jesus came into our world initially as a suffering servant. He will come again as a conquering king. The final book of the New Testament records visions God gave the apostle John about the future. Many are difficult to understand, but one that is fairly clear portrays Jesus as the triumphant king:

> Then I saw Heaven open wide—and oh! a white horse and its Rider.
> The Rider, named Faithful and True, judges and makes war in

pure righteousness. His eyes are a blaze of fire, on his head many
crowns. He has a Name inscribed that's known only to himself.
He is dressed in a robe soaked with blood, and he is addressed as
"Word of God." The armies of Heaven, mounted on white horses and
dressed in dazzling white linen, follow him. A sharp sword comes
out of his mouth so he can subdue the nations, then rule them with
a rod of iron. He treads the winepress of the raging wrath of God,
the Sovereign-Strong. On his robe and thigh is written, KING OF KINGS,
LORD OF LORDS.

REVELATION 19:11-16

Q7. As you read this passage, what do you see? How does it make you feel?

Q8. What are the possible responses people might have to Jesus' return as a king?

It may not appear at this moment that Jesus is in control of the world
and its events. Yet the Bible teaches that nothing that happens today or
tomorrow is outside the loving authority of Christ. Today Christ rules
unseen, visible only to those who have placed themselves in faith under
His authority. Someday, His authority will be visible to all.

SUMMARY

Christ is the focus of history. Everything finds its fulfillment in Him.
He is the source and sustainer of life. Our journey finds its meaning,
purpose, and destination in Him. Christ is the center around which we
find our place, the explanation of the invisible God, and the gracious
leader for those who choose to follow Him.

PRAYER

Thank You, Lord, for giving me a new center for my life. I need You as my anchor, my foundation, my compass. I have a tendency to drift in the wind, to drift off course under the pressures of daily living. I thank You for Your presence and patience to guide my journey through the uncharted waters ahead. Help me keep my eyes on You rather than on the circumstances that come my way.

NEW COMPANIONSHIP

You are not alone as you travel this journey.
God goes before you, He walks beside you, and He lives within you.
Nothing can separate you from Him. The journey involves learning
to recognize His companionship and loving presence.

*God can do anything, you know—far more than you could
ever imagine or guess or request in your wildest dreams!
He does it not by pushing us around but by working within us,
his Spirit deeply and gently within us.*

EPHESIANS 3:20

TO UNDERSTAND the awesome reality of having the God of the universe as your companion on this journey will require a look at three aspects of His companionship. First is the reality that God is not against you, but for you. He is on your side. Second, God is with you, coming alongside you as your constant companion, guide, and coach. He knows the route, the hazards, and the beautiful vistas you'll encounter along the way. His promise to be with you is one of the most repeated concepts in Scripture. Third, God is actually *in* you by His Spirit, bringing an intimacy that is closer than anything you have ever known.

HE IS FOR US

In Luke 15:11-32, we find one of the most familiar stories in the Bible, a story Rembrandt captured in his classic painting *The Return of the*

Prodigal Son. Among the story's many lessons is the persistent love of the father. The story begins like this:

> There was once a man who had two sons. The younger said to his father, "Father, I want right now what's coming to me."
> So the father divided the property between them. It wasn't long before the younger son packed his bags and left for a distant country. There, undisciplined and dissipated, he wasted everything he had.
> **LUKE 15:11-13**

Q1. **What might have motivated the son to claim his inheritance and leave home?**

The story continues:

> After he had gone through all his money, there was a bad famine all through that country and he began to hurt. He signed on with a citizen there who assigned him to his fields to slop the pigs. He was so hungry he would have eaten the corncobs in the pig slop, but no one would give him any.
> That brought him to his senses. He said, "All those farmhands working for my father sit down to three meals a day, and here I am starving to death. I'm going back to my father. I'll say to him, Father, I've sinned against God, I've sinned before you; I don't deserve to be called your son. Take me on as a hired hand."
> **LUKE 15:14-19**

Q2. **What changes occurred in the son during this part of the story?**

Jesus concluded the story with His point about unconditional love:

He got right up and went home to his father.

When he was still a long way off, his father saw him. His heart pounding, he ran out, embraced him, and kissed him. The son started his speech: "Father, I've sinned against God, I've sinned before you; I don't deserve to be called your son ever again."

But the father wasn't listening. He was calling to the servants, "Quick. Bring a clean set of clothes and dress him. Put the family ring on his finger and sandals on his feet. Then get a grain-fed heifer and roast it. We're going to feast! We're going to have a wonderful time! My son is here—given up for dead and now alive! Given up for lost and now found!" And they began to have a wonderful time.

All this time his older son was out in the field. When the day's work was done he came in. As he approached the house, he heard the music and dancing. Calling over one of the houseboys, he asked what was going on. He told him, "Your brother came home. Your father has ordered a feast—barbecued beef!—because he has him home safe and sound."

The older brother stalked off in an angry sulk and refused to join in. His father came out and tried to talk to him, but he wouldn't listen. The son said, "Look how many years I've stayed here serving you, never giving you one moment of grief, but have you ever thrown a party for me and my friends? Then this son of yours who has thrown away your money on whores shows up and you go all out with a feast!"

His father said, "Son, you don't understand. You're with me all the time, and everything that is mine is yours—but this is a wonderful time, and we had to celebrate. This brother of yours was dead, and he's alive! He was lost, and he's found!"

LUKE 15:20-32

Q3. If you had been the father, how would you have reacted? How did the father act? Why?

Q4. Compare the response of the elder brother to that of the father.

This story helps us see God's persistent love for His children. People often come to faith in Christ and find forgiveness from their past sin but secretly doubt if God is really *for* them. They believe He accepts them but can't imagine He would want to throw them a party. They wonder if there is a hidden catch. They wonder if God is waiting to see if they will really prove their merit or sincerity. They wonder if perhaps they need to work off some of the debt. The idea that God is throwing an extravagant party just for them—just because they came home—is humbling and hard to believe. In Romans 8:31, 38-39 (NASB), Paul expressed it this way:

> What then shall we say to these things? If God is for us, who is against us? . . . For I am convinced that neither death, nor life, nor angels, nor principalities, nor things present, nor things to come, nor powers, nor height, nor depth, nor any other created thing, will be able to separate us from the love of God, which is in Christ Jesus our Lord.

Q5. What thoughts or beliefs make it difficult for you to experience God's love?

Q6. If you really believed that nothing could separate you from God's love, how would you live your life?

Satan will tempt you to doubt that God is on your side. He will remind you of failures, weaknesses, inconsistencies, and unkept promises. He wants you to doubt the love of God and God's faithfulness to you. When those thoughts enter your mind, review this great truth: Personal faith in Christ guarantees God's total acceptance. God is now for you as He is for Christ Himself. You travel this journey with God as your champion and companion.

HE IS WITH US

When our youngest son was about four, we built a home on a few acres that had a pond and some timber. One evening as the sun was going down, I (Ron) asked him if he would like to go for a walk in the woods. With the enthusiasm common to that age, he ran ahead of me until we crossed the dam and approached the edge of the woods. As we approached the tree line, he dropped back and only reluctantly followed me.

I leaned down and asked, "Son, are you afraid?" He nodded his head immediately. "What are you afraid of?" He thought for a moment and said, "The bears!"

I knew it was irrelevant at that moment to inform him that there had not been a bear in these woods for more than two hundred years. But I did reach down and take his hand in mine. The transformation was immediate. Reluctance was replaced by enthusiasm, fear was replaced by courage, and silence was replaced by laughter. The difference was the assurance of my presence.

Along our faith journey, we will face the real and imaginary "bears" of life. Knowing that God has reached down and taken our hand can mean the difference between fear and peace, between hesitancy and courage.

At the very beginning of the New Testament when God announced the birth of Christ, He called Him Emmanuel, which means "God with us." And when Christ was about to leave His disciples after His resurrection, He gave them instructions that ended with a promise:

> Go out and train everyone you meet, far and near, in this way
> of life, marking them by baptism in the threefold name: Father,
> Son, and Holy Spirit. Then instruct them in the practice of all I
> have commanded you. I'll be with you as you do this, day after
> day after day, right up to the end of the age.
>
> **MATTHEW 28:19-20**

Q7. **What is the promise in this passage?**

Q8. **Describe an experience in your life when someone's presence made a difference. How did it help you?**

HE IS IN US

While it is relatively easy to understand that God is for us and beside us, the amazing concept that God is also in us is a little more difficult to comprehend. Paul wrote in Colossians 1:26-27,

> This mystery has been kept in the dark for a long time, but
> now it's out in the open. God wanted everyone, not just Jews,
> to know this rich and glorious secret inside and out, regardless
> of their background, regardless of their religious standing. The

mystery in a nutshell is just this: Christ is in you, so therefore you can look forward to sharing in God's glory. It's that simple. That is the substance of our Message.

In the Old Testament times, God's presence was confined to a building or structure (called the Tabernacle or Temple). Those serious about worshiping God could go there to meet with and experience the presence of God.

In the period of history covered by the New Testament Gospels (the first four books), God was present in Christ. Yet Christ was limited in space by a physical body. Amazing as His life was during His thirty-plus years on earth, only a few people experienced His presence. His whole life was confined to the geography of modern-day Israel.

The week before His crucifixion and resurrection, Jesus told His disciples that He was going away but that He would send His Spirit to live in them. The book of Acts in the New Testament records some of the dramatic changes that took place when His Spirit took up residence in the lives of believers.

The apostle Paul put it this way in 1 Corinthians 3:16: "You realize, don't you, that you are the temple of God, and God himself is present in you?" He explained it further in Ephesians 1:13-14 (NLT):

And now you Gentiles have also heard the truth, the Good News that God saves you. And when you believed in Christ, he identified you as his own by giving you the Holy Spirit, whom he promised long ago. The Spirit is God's guarantee that he will give us the inheritance he promised and that he has purchased us to be his own people. He did this so we would praise and glorify him.

Q9. **According to this passage, what are the results of being given the Holy Spirit?**

Because we now have His Spirit within us, we don't have to go to a particular place to experience God's presence. His presence is dramatically exposed in the lives of every follower of Christ. We are in fact little temples—each one of us a center of worship and divine presence.

Q10. **Summarize what you have learned about God being:**

- For you

- With you

- In you

SUMMARY

Christ is now our constant companion. He goes before us, walks beside us, and lives within us. He knows the path, the destination, and all the hazards ahead. He is our constant defender and promoter. He is for us, with us, and in us.

PRAYER

Thank You, Lord, for being my greatest fan. Your love for me is beyond my comprehension. Your presence within me is my comfort and joy. I know that You will never leave, abandon, or desert me. There is no place I can go where You will not guide and comfort me. Thank You for sending Your Spirit to live and dwell in my life, turning my humble body into a temple of God.

NEW CLOTHES

As we continue on our journey, God's plan is to change us to be like Christ. This change includes putting on a new wardrobe that reflects who we are in Christ. But before we put on new clothes, we must take off the old.

Now you're dressed in a new wardrobe. Every item of your new way of life is custom-made by the Creator, with his label on it. All the old fashions are now obsolete.

COLOSSIANS 3:10

WHILE ATTENDING a conference at Callaway Gardens in Georgia a few years ago, we took a walking tour through a large tropical environment where butterflies were raised. The brilliant colors of the numerous butterflies were a sensory delight. It is hard to imagine that such beauty began as fuzzy, dull caterpillars. Yet through the process of metamorphosis, caterpillars become butterflies. One form is exchanged for another.

Just as a caterpillar is changed to a butterfly, we are changed by God, an inside-out process that exchanges old traits and habits for new ones. Traits such as anger, wrath, and slander are replaced with compassion, kindness, and humility. We are being changed into the image of Christ one day at a time.

NEW IMAGE

Our change, or metamorphosis, comes through the presence and power of the Holy Spirit who now lives in us. As we cooperate with Him, He works within our minds and hearts to transform us to reflect the family image, the image of Christ.

Jesus said in Luke 6:40, "A pupil is not above his teacher; but everyone, after he has been fully trained, will be like his teacher" (NASB). When Christ is our teacher, we will become like Him. Paul put it this way in 2 Corinthians 3:18: "All of us who have had that veil removed can see and reflect the glory of the Lord. And the Lord—who is the Spirit—makes us more and more like him as we are changed into his glorious image" (NLT).

Q1.   What is the image that God is perfecting in us?

Initially, Christ's followers were called "disciples." But as the message spread into the Roman Empire, Christ's followers were called "followers of the Way" and eventually "Christians," which meant "Christlike ones." Today, the term *Christian* has lost much of that original meaning. But God's purpose remains the same: to develop a people who reflect the nature and image of His Son. While we each maintain our unique personality, we are expected to exhibit the character, values, and beliefs of Christ in our daily lives and interactions with other people.

CHANGED INSIDE AND OUT

Because Jesus is the exact representation of God, when we observe His life in the Gospels, we see not only what God is like but also what *we* are to be like. In Ephesians 4:22-24, Paul stated,

Since, then, we do not have the excuse of ignorance, everything—
and I do mean everything—connected with that old way of life has
to go. It's rotten through and through. Get rid of it! And then take
on an entirely new way of life—a God-fashioned life, a life renewed
from the inside and working itself into your conduct as God
accurately reproduces his character in you.

**Q2. What do these verses say about how you are to relate to your old way
of life?**

Although changing our behavior can be beneficial in and of itself, it can
still leave our hearts untouched. Throughout my life, as I (Ron) became
aware of anger's detrimental effect on various relationships, I learned
helpful techniques to control my anger. I learned to avoid those things
that triggered angry outbursts. I mastered techniques to control the
expression of my anger at critical moments. But I would still get angry.
I saw that behavior modification was not enough.

A key part of inside-out change is the work of the Holy Spirit. Paul
referred to this in Galatians 5:22-23 as follows: "But when the Holy
Spirit controls our lives he will produce this kind of fruit in us: love,
joy, peace, patience, kindness, goodness, faithfulness, gentleness and self-
control" (TLB).

Q3. What does it mean that the Holy Spirit "controls our lives"?

Inside-out change also involves cooperation with the Holy Spirit. Paul
said in Romans 12:1-2,

So here's what I want you to do, God helping you: Take your everyday, ordinary life—your sleeping, eating, going-to-work, and walking-around life—and place it before God as an offering. Embracing what God does for you is the best thing you can do for him. Don't become so well-adjusted to your culture that you fit into it without even thinking. Instead, fix your attention on God. You'll be changed from the inside out. Readily recognize what he wants from you, and quickly respond to it. Unlike the culture around you, always dragging you down to its level of immaturity, God brings the best out of you, develops well-formed maturity in you.

Q4. Based on this passage, what does God desire to do in you? What is your role?

God wanted to bring about real change in my life that was much deeper than simply controlling my anger. He desires change that touches our values, beliefs, and character, as well as our actions. As I prayed about this, I also began to memorize verses from the Bible that gave God's perspective on anger. The Holy Spirit took those truths and began to place them in my mind and heart to make me more patient on the inside and less angry on the outside. Real change began to take place. As we cooperate with God's Spirit within us, we become more of a true reflection of Christ. Real change happens from the inside out.

This change takes time, understanding, faith, and obedience. Like gardeners, we don't control the growth process, but we can make sure we have the right mix of water, soil, and sun. Allowing your mind to soak up the truth of Scripture is like letting a plant soak up the nutrients it needs to be healthy.

God wants this inner change or transformation to be comprehensive—affecting our minds, hearts, and wills. He wants to bring your will and emotions in line with His nature. As you cooperate with His Spirit, God powerfully changes you from the inside out.

Memorizing Scripture can help you change from the inside out. See appendix 3 for help in how to memorize Scripture effectively.

WHAT TO REMOVE

If we are to "dress for success," we first need to get rid of our old clothes that are ill-fitting, out of style, ragged, and worn out. Our old way of life represents behaviors and values that are ill-fitting for Kingdom living. In Colossians 3:5-8, Paul identified some of the "old clothes" that need to be removed:

> And that means killing off everything connected with that way of death: sexual promiscuity, impurity, lust, doing whatever you feel like whenever you feel like it, and grabbing whatever attracts your fancy. That's a life shaped by things and feelings instead of by God. It's because of this kind of thing that God is about to explode in anger. It wasn't long ago that you were doing all that stuff and not knowing any better. But you know better now, so make sure it's all gone for good: bad temper, irritability, meanness, profanity, dirty talk.

Q5. **What old clothes do you need to remove?**

WHAT TO PUT ON

Getting rid of those old clothes is often difficult and takes time. But the effort is worthwhile because the wardrobe God has for you is designer quality and appropriate for your journey. The longer you walk with Christ, the better the new clothes fit and feel. Paul said in Colossians 3:9-14,

Don't lie to one another. You're done with that old life. It's like a
filthy set of ill-fitting clothes you've stripped off and put in the fire.
Now you're dressed in a new wardrobe. Every item of your new
way of life is custom-made by the Creator, with his label on it. All
the old fashions are now obsolete. Words like Jewish and non-
Jewish, religious and irreligious, insider and outsider, uncivilized
and uncouth, slave and free, mean nothing. From now on everyone
is defined by Christ, everyone is included in Christ.

So, chosen by God for this new life of love, dress in the wardrobe God picked out for you: compassion, kindness, humility, quiet
strength, discipline. Be even-tempered, content with second place,
quick to forgive an offense. Forgive as quickly and completely as the
Master forgave you. And regardless of what else you put on, wear
love. It's your basic, all-purpose garment. Never be without it.

Q6. **List three items included in this passage that you will use to make up
your new wardrobe.**

Q7. **What is the one basic "garment" that fits you for the journey, regardless
of the weather or terrain?**

Q8. **Why is love fundamental to any outfit you might choose?**

From suits and ties to ripped jeans and T-shirts, people are identified
or judged (right or wrong) by the clothes they wear. In John 13:34-35,
Jesus told His disciples that the world would judge how close they were

to Him based on how well they were clothed with love toward one another. He said, "Let me give you a new command: Love one another. In the same way I loved you, you love one another. This is how everyone will recognize that you are my disciples—when they see the love you have for each other."

The most distinctive mark of a Christ follower is how he or she expresses love. Loving in the same way Christ loved us involves giving while expecting nothing in return.

SUMMARY

As we travel the journey with Christ, we will become like Him. We will reflect His nature and character. God has a new wardrobe for us to put on that reflects our new nature. It involves both taking off our old habits and patterns of behavior and putting on new ones. It is more than just behavior modification, however. It is a change from the inside out.

PRAYER

Lord, change me today to look more like You. Replace the discord of my heart with the melody of Your Spirit. May my life today touch others with the reality of Your love. Change me by Your power so that the only possible explanation of who I am becoming is the touch of Your presence.

NEW CALLING

God has called us to experience an awesome life. He invites us to join Him in accomplishing His purposes. Life is not meager, dull, or boring when we follow Christ. He is doing something big and wants us to be a part. Knowing and participating in what God is doing will make your journey significant.

*You were all called to travel on the same road and in the same direction,
so stay together, both outwardly and inwardly.*

EPHESIANS 4:4

ON A TRIP TO CHINA, I (Ron) stopped in a factory where artisans were weaving silk rugs by hand on wooden looms. The weaver was constantly adding new yarn as the color and pattern changed. Looking over the weaver's shoulder, the rug was unimpressive. Knots were prominent, and the pattern was obscured. But when I walked around the loom and saw the rug from the other side, its beauty was obvious. It is now hanging on a wall in our living room!

God is the divine artisan who is weaving our life story into a beautiful pattern. From one side we see the knots and scars, but God is able to take each experience and fashion a work of art.

Coming to faith in Christ brings with it a new start and a new direction. We are no longer left to wander aimlessly. Christ has called us on a path of purpose. His plan for us began before the world was created.

The word *calling* means a mission, work, or vocation. The Bible teaches that man, created in the image of God, has a mission. Through Christ we can discover our mission and join Him in accomplishing it. In the Old Testament, God reminded His family of their call to an extraordinary life. This is what He said in Jeremiah 29:11: "I know what I'm doing. I have it all planned out—plans to take care of you, not abandon you, plans to give you the future you hope for." Jesus expressed the same idea in the New Testament in John 10:10: "I came so they can have real and eternal life, more and better life than they ever dreamed of."

God wants us to know where we are going. He has given us all an outline of what our journey will involve. The details of His plan will be filled in as we go along, but our calling from God is clear. As you understand and participate in His calling, you will enjoy tastes of the abundant life Jesus promised. The apostle Paul was so convinced of this that it became part of his prayer for the new believers in Ephesus. In Ephesians 1:17-18 he said, "I ask—ask the God of our Master, Jesus Christ, the God of glory—to make you intelligent and discerning in knowing him personally, your eyes focused and clear, so that you can see exactly what it is he is calling you to do, grasp the immensity of this glorious way of life he has for his followers."

CALLED TO EXPERIENCE GOD'S DIVINE LOVE

Paul began his letter to the new believers in Ephesus by reminding them that, from the beginning, God has made us the center of His love. In Ephesians 1:4, Paul said, "Long before he laid down earth's foundations, he had us in mind, had settled on us as the focus of his love."

God wants to touch people with His incredible love. God wants us to know from deep, personal experience that He loves us with a love that is beyond our wildest imagination. Paul's prayer for the new believers in Ephesus included a plea to seek out that kind of love:

I ask him to strengthen you by his Spirit—not a brute strength but a glorious inner strength—that Christ will live in you as you open the door and invite him in. And I ask him that with both feet planted firmly on love, you'll be able to take in with all followers of Jesus the extravagant dimensions of Christ's love. Reach out and experience the breadth! Test its length! Plumb the depths! Rise to the heights! Live full lives, full in the fullness of God.

EPHESIANS 3:16-19

Q1.   Write Paul's prayer in your own words.

Knowing something as a fact and experiencing it as a personal reality can be worlds apart. You probably have seen pictures of the earth taken from inside one of NASA's shuttles. You may have heard the astronauts' excitement as they attempted to explain what it's like to look at our planet from hundreds of miles away in space. Yet no explanation or picture can substitute for actually being there. We can know *about* it, but the astronauts know by experience.

In the same way, you can read about God's love, hear it described, and even know people who have experienced it. You can believe that God loves you without experiencing it personally. God wants you to know His love not simply by looking at Him, but by being closely involved with Him. Take a look at what Ephesians 5:1-2 says:

Watch what God does, and then you do it, like children who learn proper behavior from their parents. Mostly what God does is love you. Keep company with him and learn a life of love. Observe how Christ loved us. His love was not cautious but extravagant. He didn't love in order to get something from us but to give everything of himself to us. Love like that.

Q2. What do these verses say to you about God's love?

Q3. What is your response to God's love?

CALLED TO PERSONAL SPIRITUAL MATURITY

God desires followers who are holy, mature, and strong in their life of faith. But we don't start out that way. Spiritual maturity is a matter of time and of understanding God's Word and obeying it.

Paul said we begin our faith journey as infants and grow into maturity. He used this familiar metaphor to help us understand the process that God is taking us through. Even as young children, we think and act in a way that is appropriate for our age. But as we mature, we learn to act differently. Each stage of development along the way is critical.

Maturity in our spiritual journey results from three things:

1. Understanding God's Word
2. Applying God's truth to our lives
3. Growing over time

Reading the Bible is an important part of the growth process for a new follower of Christ. The apostle Peter wrote in 1 Peter 2:2, "Like newborn babies, long for the pure milk of the word, so that by it you may grow in respect to salvation" (NASB). And Jesus said in Matthew 4:4, "It is written, 'MAN SHALL NOT LIVE ON BREAD ALONE, BUT ON EVERY WORD THAT PROCEEDS OUT OF THE MOUTH OF GOD'" (NASB). (For help in how to read the Bible, see appendix 3.)

Paul stated the following in Ephesians 4:12-15:

[God enables leaders] to train Christ's followers in skilled servant work, working within Christ's body, the church, until we're all moving rhythmically and easily with each other, efficient and graceful in response to God's Son, fully mature adults, fully developed within and without, fully alive like Christ. No prolonged infancies among us, please. We'll not tolerate babes in the woods, small children who are an easy mark for impostors. God wants us to grow up, to know the whole truth and tell it in love—like Christ in everything. We take our lead from Christ, who is the source of everything we do.

Q4. **How do these verses describe adults who are mature in faith?**

Q5. **What do the verses say about those who remain infants in their faith?**

CALLED TO AUTHENTIC COMMUNITY WITH OTHERS

God is building a community of faith where all people belong, regardless of their past. There are no divisions or special classes in this community. Regardless of what or who we were, where we have come from, or how we got here, the ground is level for us who are in Christ. Paul made this point very clear in Ephesians 2:18-20:

He treated us as equals, and so made us equals. Through him we both share the same Spirit and have equal access to the Father.
   That's plain enough, isn't it? You're no longer wandering exiles. This kingdom of faith is now your home country. You're no longer strangers or outsiders. You *belong* here, with as much right to the

name Christian as anyone. God is building a home. He's using us all—irrespective of how we got here—in what he is building. He used the apostles and prophets for the foundation. Now he's using you, fitting you in brick by brick, stone by stone, with Christ Jesus as the cornerstone.

Q6. What do these verses say is true about each person who has come to Christ by faith?

The community of faith is a place where everyone is welcome and accepted. It's a family that crosses ethnic and social boundaries. God's design for this community, called the church, is to create a place where everyone involved experiences mutual acceptance and harmony.

As part of God's family, we each have a contribution to make to the lives of others. Our relationship with Christ will naturally overflow into loving service to others. Paul wrote in Ephesians 2:10, "No, we neither make nor save ourselves. God does both the making and saving. He creates each of us by Christ Jesus to join him in the work he does, the good work he has gotten ready for us to do, work we had better be doing."

Q7. What do you think Paul had in mind when he referred to "the work he does"?

Community is experienced not only in large group settings, usually called worship or celebration services, but also in small groups and mentoring relationships. As you begin your journey, seek out a variety of ways to experience this community.

You are a significant and essential part of God's community. Because you are unique, no one can take your place. The more you live and learn on your journey, the more you will discover where you fit within the community of Christ.

Q8. Where can you go to find a community for worship and teaching?

SUMMARY

We are created and called to God's purposes. His plans go beyond this life into eternity. We are made by God and for God. God has called us to know His love deeply, to grow toward maturity personally, to live in community authentically, and to serve others willingly.

PRAYER

Nothing compares to finding my ultimate purpose in You, God. Help me lay aside my trivial pursuits and catch hold of Your grand plan. Help me align my life with the eternal design that is at work and that will ultimately fill the universe. Take my best attempt at finger painting and create a work of art on the canvas of human lives that You allow me to touch. Let Your joy fill my heart as You produce spiritual fruit in and through me.

SUMMARY

USE THE FOLLOWING CHART to review the lessons you have just completed. You may want to show someone else what you have been learning about your journey with Christ.

LESSON	KEY QUESTION	KEY VERSE	KEY CONCEPTS
New Connection	Is my relationship with God really different?	Ephesians 2:7	Because of Christ I am (1) loved by the Father, (2) freed by the Son, and (3) certified by the Spirit.
New Creation	Who am I?	2 Corinthians 5:17	In Christ I am (1) alive, (2) a saint, (3) forgiven, (4) a citizen of God's Kingdom, and (5) a member of God's family.
New Center	Who's in control?	Colossians 1:15	Christ is (1) the center of my world, (2) the revelation of God, and (3) the leader of my life.
New Companionship	Who is walking with me on this journey?	Ephesians 3:20	Christ is (1) for me, (2) with me, and (3) in me.
New Clothes	What attitudes and actions should I "wear"?	Colossians 3:10	Christ is creating in me (1) the family image, (2) an inside-out change, and (3) an appropriate wardrobe.
New Calling	Where am I going?	Ephesians 4:4	Christ calls me to experience (1) divine love, (2) spiritual maturity, (3) authentic community, and (4) personal contribution.

JESUS THE TRUTH

MY (MARY'S) MOTHER OWNED a grand piano that was built in 1925 by the Bush and Lane Piano Company of Michigan. It was her most prized possession. The piano had a black lacquer finish, ivory keys, and a rich sound. I learned to play the piano on this grand instrument, spending countless hours practicing throughout high school. Great memories and feelings were etched deep into my heart over those years.

Later, the piano was unwisely stored in a damp basement for many years. The dampness took a toll. The once-beautiful finish rippled, the ivory keys chipped, and the strings slacked. When it was recovered from the basement, the piano had to be completely rebuilt and refinished. After months of work by an expert craftsman, it was completely restored with new pins, felts, hammers, keys, and strings. And the finish was reconditioned to a beautiful mahogany elegance.

A few years ago I inherited the piano, and we carefully moved it to our new home in Kansas City—a home that had been designed with a large great room specifically to accommodate this anticipated family heirloom.

So how much is this piano worth? There are several factors that determine the value of the instrument. One is the reputation of the original makers. Were they highly skilled craftsmen? Another factor is the musical tone. Does it produce quality sound? A third factor is previous ownership. Who has previously owned or played it? A final factor is the price paid for it. How much is someone willing to pay?

In many ways, we are like this grand piano. We have been designed and made by the creator of the universe. We are the result of quality workmanship and capable of beautiful music. We have been repurchased by the very life of Christ and are now being restored under His ownership. We are God's priceless heirlooms. And there is a special place in His home designed just for us.

But how do we view ourselves? Do we see ourselves as priceless? Do we really believe we have great personal worth to God . . . to others . . . to ourselves? Or do we view ourselves as garage sale merchandise? Some people put a lot of effort into trying to look successful and important. Others, burdened with past mistakes, see themselves as expendable and worthless.

The following study will explore who we are in light of our relationship with God. We will discover the truth of our value as we look at our new identity in Christ. Much of what we will learn comes from the Gospel of John.

The Gospel of John was written by one of the twelve original disciples who was also one of Jesus' three closest friends. In his Gospel, John focused primarily on Jesus' teachings.

As you continue your walk, you will study the following word pictures to help you understand who you are in Christ:

- His Workmanship
- His Sheep
- His Child
- His Follower
- His Branch
- His Dwelling Place

LESSON 7

HIS WORKMANSHIP

God places great value on us because we are uniquely made in His image.
Even though that image has been marred and distorted, He paid the ultimate
price to gain the right to restore us once again to beauty and significance.

Yet you, LORD, are our Father.
We are the clay, you are the potter;
we are all the work of your hand.

ISAIAH 64:8, NIV

THE BIBLE CLEARLY CLAIMS that out of all God created, humanity
uniquely shares "His image." The writer of Psalm 139 says, "I praise you
because I am fearfully and wonderfully made; your works are wonderful,
I know that full well" (verse 14, NIV). In an earlier psalm he writes,

When I consider your heavens,
    the work of your fingers,
the moon and the stars,
    which you have set in place,
what is man that you are mindful of him,
    the son of man that you care for him?
You made him a little lower than the heavenly beings
    and crowned him with glory and honor.

PSALM 8:3-5, NIV

Our culture tends to value people for their looks, abilities, or performance. But God values us for who we are. One of the traits that made Jesus attractive was His countercultural way of giving value and honor to everyone. The wealthy or poor, the healthy or sick, the elite or the ordinary—each person felt honor and dignity in His presence.

God wants us to know that we are stamped with His likeness from the very beginning. We may be marred and scarred; we may need major refinishing, but we are still uniquely created in His divine image.

UNIQUELY MADE

Q1.   What does the following passage say about Christ?

> In the beginning the Word already existed.
>> The Word was with God,
>> and the Word was God.
> He existed in the beginning with God.
> God created everything through him,
>> and nothing was created except through him.
>
> **JOHN 1:1-3, NLT**

Q2.   Read Genesis 1:20-28 and 2:7. According to these verses, what is the difference between the way God made the animals and the way He made human beings? What does this imply about our value?

Q3.   What do you think it means to be created in God's image? How are we like God? How are we not like God?

Q4. How does the truth that you are created in God's image affect the value you attribute to yourself?

Read what the Bible says about God's creative process in Psalm 139:13-16 (NIV):

> For you created my inmost being;
>   you knit me together in my mother's womb.
> I praise you because I am fearfully and
>   wonderfully made;
>   your works are wonderful,
>   I know that full well.
> My frame was not hidden from you
>   when I was made in the secret place.
> When I was woven together in the depths
>   of the earth,
>   your eyes saw my unformed body.
> All the days ordained for me
>   were written in your book
>   before one of them came to be.

Q5. What is implied in this passage about our unique design?

ULTIMATE VALUE

King David was a prominent Old Testament character. He first was a shepherd, next became a fugitive, and finally ruled as the greatest king of Israel. Besides being a great warrior, he wrote poetry, some of which is recorded in the Old Testament book of Psalms.

Q6. Read the following passage and circle what King David said about the importance of people in relation to the rest of creation.

O LORD, our Lord,
how majestic is your name in all the earth!
You have set your glory
above the heavens.
From the lips of children and infants
you have ordained praise
because of your enemies,
to silence the foe and the avenger.
When I consider your heavens,
the work of your fingers,
the moon and the stars,
which you have set in place,
what is man that you are mindful of him,
the son of man that you care for him?
You made him a little lower than the heavenly beings
and crowned him with glory and honor.
You made him ruler over the works of your hands;
you put everything under his feet:
all flocks and herds,
and the beasts of the field,
the birds of the air,
and the fish of the sea,
all that swim the paths of the seas.
O LORD, our Lord,
how majestic is your name in all the earth!

PSALM 8:1-9, NIV

Q7. Look up the following verses in your Bible and notice how Jesus placed value on people by the way He treated them. Compare this with the value placed on the same people by others.

PASSAGE	JESUS' VIEW	OTHERS' VIEW
Little children (Mark 10:13-16)		
An immoral woman (John 4:7-10, 16-18, 27)		
A blind man (Mark 10:46-52)		

Although we have been created in God's divine image, that image has been marred and distorted. Yet God still values us. In Luke 4:18-19, Jesus said,

> God's Spirit is on me;
>   he's chosen me to preach the Message of good news to the poor,
> Sent me to announce pardon to prisoners and
>   recovery of sight to the blind,
> To set the burdened and battered free,
>   to announce, "This is God's year to act!"

Q8. Based on this passage, how did Jesus illustrate the value He placed on broken people?

Q9. How do you respond to the idea that you were handcrafted by God and therefore are very valuable?

_____ This is a new idea and difficult to believe.

_____ The idea appeals to me, but I have many more questions.

_____ I have heard this before, but I still struggle with seeing myself as valuable.

_____ I believe this truth, but the circumstances of life make it easy to forget.

_____ I am grateful God made me, and His handiwork gives me a great sense of value.

_____ Other:

Q10. **Finish this sentence with the truths you have discovered from your study: Because I am God's workmanship, created in His image . . .**

SUMMARY

In all of God's creation, people are unique. When God created us, He made us for a personal relationship with Himself. Even though we have missed the mark of God's moral standards, resulting in a distortion of the original design, God still values us. Jesus Christ enables us to be new people. As new people, we are able to experience a rich relationship with our Creator God.

PRAYER

Dear God, Your creation is awesome. The incredible size, variety, and complexity of all You have made overwhelms me. When I read in the Bible that You made me special and desire a close relationship with me, I can hardly believe it. Thank You for sending Jesus to put me back together and to enable me to develop a close relationship with You.

HIS SHEEP

The Good Shepherd, Jesus, values us as His sheep. He guides, protects, and cares for us as a shepherd would guide, protect, and care for his most prized possession.

*I am the good shepherd. The good shepherd
lays down his life for the sheep.*

JOHN 10:11, NIV

SHEEP WERE A SIGNIFICANT agricultural resource in Jesus' culture. It is no accident, then, that Jesus used the image of sheep and a shepherd to teach us about our true identity and our value to Him.

When I (Ron) picture a sheep ranch in the western United States, I imagine green, fenced-in pastures with small ponds. I picture a scene where dogs or perhaps even ranchers on all-terrain vehicles circle around the sheep to guide them into a corral for shearing. This, however, is not the image Jesus had in mind when He called Himself the Good Shepherd in John 10.

Phillip Keller was born in East Africa and was a shepherd himself. In his book *A Shepherd Looks at the Good Shepherd*,[1] he provides a cultural background for understanding Jesus' analogy of shepherd and sheep. According to Keller, a good shepherd rises early in the morning to get his sheep from the sheepfold. The fold, an enclosure usually built of rock or thornbush, is intended to protect the sheep from wild animals or thieves. It is not, however, a healthy place due to the buildup of debris and dung. Because of this, the shepherd never leaves his sheep in the fold any longer than necessary. He also wants to get the sheep out early in the morning before the dew has evaporated because this is often the only moisture available for the flock.

Upon the shepherd's arrival, he calls each one of his sheep by name. The sheep do not have common names like we might use today. Rather, each one has a name that reflects its personal history. For example, one might be "The one born in the dry riverbed" or "The beautiful lamb for whom I traded two pots of honey." The sheep recognize the shepherd's voice and respond quickly because they have associated his voice with attention and benefits. They will not, however, respond to the voice of a stranger. Upon hearing their names, the sheep run to their master eagerly, awaiting the expected caressing, hugs, and words of endearment. The shepherd also scrutinizes each sheep carefully to be sure it is free of disease or injury.

Once the flock is together, the shepherd leads them by his voice. The Middle Eastern shepherd does not use dogs or other animals to "drive" the sheep as we do cattle. Rather, he walks in front of them and leads them to rich pastures and clean water. These are available only if the shepherd manages the land well. The shepherd's reputation is based on his expert management of both his flock and his pastures that enable his sheep to flourish.

A particularly important difference between the sheep ranches of today and the shepherding of Jesus' day is the profound and intimate relationship between shepherd and sheep. Keller observed this difference in the people of East Africa, where sheep literally grow up in the family household. They are cuddled, hugged, fed, and loved just like the shepherd's own children. Each individual sheep is well-known from the day of its birth throughout its lifetime. The bond between shepherd and sheep is based on love and caring, not merely on monetary gain.

THE GOOD SHEPHERD

In light of this background, read John 10:1-18:

"Let me set this before you as plainly as I can. If a person climbs over or through the fence of a sheep pen instead of going through the gate, you know he's up to no good—a sheep rustler! The shepherd walks right up to the gate. The gatekeeper opens the gate to him and the sheep recognize his voice. He calls his own sheep by name and leads them out. When he gets them all out, he leads them and they follow because they are familiar with his voice. They won't follow a stranger's voice but will scatter because they aren't used to the sound of it."

Jesus told this simple story, but they had no idea what he was talking about. So he tried again. "I'll be explicit, then. I am the Gate for the sheep. All those others are up to no good—sheep stealers, every one of them. But the sheep didn't listen to them. I am the Gate. Anyone who goes through me will be cared for—will freely go in and out, and find pasture. A thief is only there to steal and kill and destroy. I came so they can have real and eternal life, more and better life than they ever dreamed of.

"I am the Good Shepherd. The Good Shepherd puts the sheep before himself, sacrifices himself if necessary. A hired man is not a real shepherd. The sheep mean nothing to him. He sees a wolf come and runs for it, leaving the sheep to be ravaged and scattered by the wolf. He's only in it for the money. The sheep don't matter to him.

"I am the Good Shepherd. I know my own sheep and my own sheep know me. In the same way, the Father knows me and I know the Father. I put the sheep before myself, sacrificing myself if necessary. You need to know that I have other sheep in addition to those in this pen. I need to gather and bring them, too. They'll also recognize my voice. Then it will be one flock, one Shepherd. This is why the Father loves me: because I freely lay down my life. And so I am free to take it up again. No one takes it from me. I lay it down of my own free will. I have the right to lay it down; I also have the right to take it up again. I received this authority personally from my Father."

Q1. Why do you think Jesus referred to Himself as the "Good Shepherd" in this passage?

Jesus said the Good Shepherd "lays down his life" for the sheep. He repeated this idea four times. When Jesus referred to laying down His life, He was referring to His death on the cross. This is later described in 1 Peter 3:18:

> That's what Christ did definitively: suffered because of others' sins, the Righteous One for the unrighteous ones. He went through it all—was put to death and then made alive—to bring us to God.

And also in John 3:16:

> This is how much God loved the world: He gave his Son, his one and only Son. And this is why: so that no one need be destroyed; by believing in him, anyone can have a whole and lasting life.

Q2. Look at the last paragraph in the John 10:1-18 passage. Describe your reaction when you read Jesus' words about His life: "No one takes it from me. I lay it down of my own free will."

Q3. What motivated Jesus to lay down His life?

Q4. Who tries to enter the fold in a way other than through the gate? Who or what do you think this person represents?

Q5. Compare the goal of the thief and the goal of the Good Shepherd.

The Bible teaches that Satan and his demonic hosts are not imaginary literary figures but real beings who oppose God. Having aligned ourselves with God by faith, we are targets of Satan's schemes and strategies. Therefore, "keep a cool head. Stay alert. The Devil is poised to pounce, and would like nothing better than to catch you napping" (1 Peter 5:8).

THE SECURE DOOR

Unlike lions or bears, sheep have no natural self-protection. They must depend entirely on the skill and power of the shepherd. In Jesus' day, shepherds often slept across the gate of the fold to protect their flock. Our identity as the sheep of Christ's flock brings with it the necessary and adequate protection of the Good Shepherd. We are as safe as He is strong. His sheep are in danger only if they step outside His protection. We must learn to rely on the protection and power of our Good Shepherd if we are to remain safe from predators and our own folly.

Q6. Why do you think Jesus called Himself the "gate" or "door" in John 10? (John 14:6 may also give some insight.)

Jesus the Good Shepherd promises to provide "real and eternal life" for His sheep (John 10:10).

Q7. **What comes to mind when you think of having "real and eternal life"?**

The analogy of God as our Shepherd is found throughout the Bible. The most familiar reference is Psalm 23. King David, who spent his youth shepherding his father's sheep, wrote the often-quoted words. His boyhood experiences later gave him great insight into his own relationship with God.

Q8. **Read Psalm 23 (NIV) and circle all the things the Shepherd does for His sheep.**

The LORD is my shepherd, I shall not be in want.
He makes me lie down in green pastures,
he leads me beside quiet waters,
he restores my soul.
He guides me in paths of righteousness
for his name's sake.
Even though I walk
through the valley of the shadow of death,
I will fear no evil,
for you are with me;
your rod and your staff,
they comfort me.
You prepare a table before me
in the presence of my enemies.
You anoint my head with oil;
my cup overflows.
Surely goodness and love will follow me

> all the days of my life,
> and I will dwell in the house of the LORD
>   forever.

Q9. **Summarize in your own words what God, your Shepherd, does for you.**

Sheep can be stubborn and fearful animals. They tend to go their own way and panic at the first sight (imagined or real) of danger. Even with a watchful shepherd, they often wander off and become vulnerable to harm.

Q10. **Why do you think we often act in a similar manner?**

Sometimes we leave the safety of the Good Shepherd out of fear. We read in 1 John 4:18 that "such love has no fear, because perfect love expels all fear. If we are afraid, it is for fear of punishment, and this shows that we have not fully experienced his perfect love" (NLT).

Believing that the Good Shepherd loves us and will protect us is key to our walk with Christ. Yet when we interpret our circumstances through the warped grid of our feelings rather than through the truth of God's Word, it is sometimes difficult to believe in that love. This is one reason why reading God's Word is important. It increases our understanding of God's love and helps us trust Him more.

Q11. **How would it change your daily life if you related to Jesus as your personal Shepherd?**

SUMMARY

Jesus is the Good Shepherd who takes the needs of His sheep seriously. He looks after those who follow Him by giving them protection, nourishment, and guidance. His death on the cross demonstrates how much He cares for His sheep. Jesus wants each person who follows Him to experience a full life, trusting Him to be a faithful Shepherd.

PRAYER

Thank You, Jesus, for being my Good Shepherd. I realize I am like a sheep that at times strays from the flock. Please forgive me when I do this. Help me to keep following You. I want to experience the full life that You promise. Thank You for Your deep love and for never giving up on me.

HIS CHILD

Through faith in Christ, we are given a new identity as children of God. We are adopted into His family with all the rights, privileges, and responsibilities of sons and daughters.

Yet to all who received him, to those who believed in his name, he gave the right to become children of God.

JOHN 1:12, NIV

BEING A CHILD OF GOD IS not simply a result of our humanity. It is a result of being adopted into His family through faith in Christ. Understanding adoption helps us appreciate our new family relationship with God and others. It tells us something about the heart of God and our new identity as members of His family.

Most men and women desire to have children. For couples who are not able to have their own children, adoption may be their only opportunity to build a family. But it doesn't have to feel like a "second-best" choice. I know several couples who have adopted children, and in each case their incredible love for these children is obvious. Their attitude, actions, and words reflect excitement, joy, and a deep appreciation for their adopted children.

↘ Adoption in our culture is expensive. Travel, prenatal care, and legal fees can make the cost prohibitive. The paperwork can stretch over months, and the emotional trauma can be exhausting. Some couples are "promised" a baby, only to learn later that the birth mother has changed her mind and decided to raise the baby herself.

So why do adoptive parents put themselves through such stress and strain? Love! The desire to pour out their affection, to care for and raise a child, no matter what the cost. The Bible tells us that when we come to Christ through faith, God adopts us into His family as His sons and daughters. We are now a part of His "forever family," as one adoption judge put it. Read what Paul had to say about this adoption in Ephesians 1:5: "Long, long ago he decided to adopt us into his family through Jesus Christ. (What pleasure he took in planning this!)"

Every person is created uniquely by the awesome workmanship of God. But even though we are created in His image, our declaration of independence has separated us from God. Created by God but spiritually separated from Him is the normal condition of humanity. Jesus' sacrifice on the cross is the price God paid to adopt us back into His family. In this lesson we will look at several implications of being adopted into God's family.

LIVING AS AN ADOPTED CHILD

Q1. What does the following passage tell us about how we become children of God?

Yet to all who received him, to those who believed in his name, he gave the right to become children of God—children born not of natural descent, nor of human decision or a husband's will, but born of God.

JOHN 1:12-13, NIV

The word *right* means "ability, privilege, capacity, competency, freedom, authority, jurisdiction, liberty, power, or strength."[1]

Q2. Read John 1:12-13 ten more times, each time substituting one of these synonyms for the word *right*. Do you gain any further insights?

The apostle John wrote some short letters (1, 2, and 3 John) in which he continued to expand on this incredible privilege of becoming God's child. Here's what he said in 1 John 3:1-3:

> What marvelous love the Father has extended to us! Just look at it—we're called children of God! That's who we really are. But that's also why the world doesn't recognize us or take us seriously, because it has no idea who he is or what he's up to.
>
> But friends, that's exactly who we are: children of God. And that's only the beginning. Who knows how we'll end up! What we know is that when Christ is openly revealed, we'll see him—and in seeing him, become like him. All of us who look forward to his Coming stay ready, with the glistening purity of Jesus' life as a model for our own.

Q3. According to John, what is God's motivation for adopting us into His family? What is the ultimate goal God has for us as His children?

John said we are not just *called* "children of God," but we actually *are* children of God. That is now our true identity. We have been given a new relationship with God and are now an intimate part of His family.

Q4. Look at the following verses and circle some of our privileges and benefits in this new relationship.

God's Spirit beckons. There are things to do and places to go! This resurrection life you received from God is not a timid, grave-tending life. It's adventurously expectant, greeting God with a childlike "What's next, Papa?" God's Spirit touches our spirits and confirms who we really are. We know who he is, and we know who we are: Father and children. And we know we are going to get what's coming to us—an unbelievable inheritance! We go through exactly what Christ goes through. If we go through the hard times with him, then we're certainly going to go through the good times with him!

ROMANS 8:14-17

LIVING WITH A LOVING FATHER

It is not surprising that when we try to understand God as our Father, we reflect on the model of our biological or "earthly" father. Yet no matter how good your relationship is or was with an earthly father, that model is inadequate. All earthly father models are flawed . . . some more than others. The concept of a father originates with God. Our physical fathers are only shadows at best of God the Father.

In a culture where fatherhood has been distorted, where we have fathering without responsibility and a name but no relationship, it is easy to miss who God is as our Father. For some, it may even be painful to think about God as their father. If you are in this position, your heavenly Father understands and cares about your struggle. Ask Him to help you overcome these emotional barriers. Remind yourself that your heavenly Father is different from your earthly father. If your emotional response to the concept of a father is negative and painful, it may be helpful to develop your "father portrait" by first just looking at the character of Jesus. Jesus is the exact representation of God. It may be easier for you to look at the character traits in Jesus to build an understanding of who God the Father is. After all, Jesus Himself said, "I and the Father are one" (John 10:30).

God wants you to have an accurate understanding of not only who you are but also who He is and how deeply He loves you. With the help of the Holy Spirit, you can gain that understanding.

Q5. Describe your picture of the ideal father.

Q6. Highlight the description of God in Psalm 103:8-13 (NIV):

The LORD is compassionate and gracious,
    slow to anger, abounding in love.
He will not always accuse,
    nor will he harbor his anger forever;
he does not treat us as our sins deserve
    or repay us according to our iniquities.
For as high as the heavens are above the earth,
    so great is his love for those who fear him;
as far as the east is from the west,
    so far has he removed our transgressions from us.
As a father has compassion on his children,
    so the LORD has compassion on those who fear him.

Q7. How might your life be different if you lived as one who truly believed this description of God?

Q8. What does the following passage say is the responsibility of a loving father? What is our responsibility as children?

Endure hardship as discipline; God is treating you as sons. For what son is not disciplined by his father? If you are not disciplined—and everyone undergoes discipline—then you are illegitimate children and not true sons. Moreover, we have all had human fathers who disciplined us and we respected them for it. How much more should we submit to the Father of our spirits and live! Our fathers disciplined us for a little while as they thought best; but God disciplines us for our good, that we may share in his holiness. No discipline seems pleasant at the time, but painful. Later on, however, it produces a harvest of righteousness and peace for those who have been trained by it.

HEBREWS 12:7-11, NIV

Q9. How do these verses describe God's discipline?

LIVING WITH OUR NEW IDENTITY

Human parents prepare their children to become independent so they can leave home and make it on their own. Our heavenly Father has a different goal.

Q10. According to the following verses, what does God desire from us? What does He promise us?

Trust in the LORD with all your heart
   and lean not on your own understanding;

in all your ways acknowledge him,
>   and he will make your paths straight.
Do not be wise in your own eyes;
>   fear the LORD and shun evil.
This will bring health to your body
>   and nourishment to your bones.

PROVERBS 3:5-8, NIV

Trust, built out of knowledge and experience, brings with it a sense of security and acceptance. God is eager to demonstrate to us that He deserves our trust.

Q11. Read the following passage and circle what God does that makes you feel secure and accepted.

God knew what he was doing from the very beginning. He decided from the outset to shape the lives of those who love him along the same lines as the life of his Son. The Son stands first in the line of humanity he restored. We see the original and intended shape of our lives there in him. After God made that decision of what his children should be like, he followed it up by calling people by name. After he called them by name, he set them on a solid basis with himself. And then, after getting them established, he stayed with them to the end, gloriously completing what he had begun.

So, what do you think? With God on our side like this, how can we lose? If God didn't hesitate to put everything on the line for us, embracing our condition and exposing himself to the worst by sending his own Son, is there anything else he wouldn't gladly and freely do for us? And who would dare tangle with God by messing with one of God's chosen? Who would dare even to point a finger? The One who died for us—who was raised to life for us!—is in the presence of God at this very moment sticking up for us. Do you think anyone is going to be able to drive a wedge between us and Christ's love for us? There is no way! Not trouble, not hard times, not hatred, not hunger, not homelessness, not bullying threats, not backstabbing, not even the worst sins listed in Scripture. . . . None of this fazes us because Jesus loves us. I'm absolutely convinced that nothing—nothing living or dead, angelic or demonic, today or tomorrow, high or low, thinkable or unthinkable—absolutely *nothing* can get between us and God's love because of the way that Jesus our Master has embraced us.

ROMANS 8:29-35, 37-39

Our identity as children of God is more than a nice idea. It is a truth that can lead to a loving, trusting, and secure relationship with God. Trust and security come from knowing we are loved and valued by someone who has our best interests in mind at all times. God loves us perfectly, working out everything in our lives for our welfare. We may not always understand what He is doing, just as a child does not always understand the decisions his father makes. The child feels secure, however, because he is confident of his father's love and commitment to provide and protect.

Trust is built not only on the integrity of the other party, but also on how well we know that person. The same is true in our relationship with our heavenly Father. The better we know Him, the easier it is to trust Him. As you continue your walk, learn about God by reading the Bible (His communication with us) and by praying (our communication with Him). Rely on Him to help you apply biblical principles to your daily life. As you experience His presence, you will learn to trust Him more.

SUMMARY

When we turn to Christ and place our faith in Him, we become a part of God's family. God's special act of adoption guarantees us full rights and privileges in His family. He makes us people of value. As His children we can experience His loving and special care.

PRAYER

What a privilege it is to address You as my Father—to think that You would even want to be known as my Father. I am only beginning to grasp all that this means. I know I am bringing a lot of baggage into this family relationship. Some of it is ignorance, some misconceptions, and some the result of my past pain and scars. Help me develop this relationship. Open the eyes of my heart so that I can grasp what it means to be a true child of a loving heavenly Father. Help me trust You with every aspect of my life.

LESSON 10

HIS FOLLOWER

Jesus has given us an incredible invitation: He invites us to follow Him. He left a timeless eternity to take on the limitations of our humanity. He demonstrated the very nature and character of God so we could know Him. And He asks us to "come and see"—to become His disciples.

Jesus said to them, "Come with me. I'll make a new kind of fisherman out of you. I'll show you how to catch men and women instead of perch and bass."

MATTHEW 4:19

I (RON) WAS ATTENDING the army's Infantry Officer Candidate School at Fort Benning. In a short six months, we were to go from privates to second lieutenants. The patch that formed our unit's identity and appeared on the left shoulder of every uniform was a sword in the middle of a shield. Over the shield were the words "Follow Me." One day it dawned on us that in a few months, we would be leading a platoon through a hostile jungle in Southeast Asia. These men's lives (and ours) would depend on our skill as leaders. So we covertly designed another unit patch. This one had the same sword and shield, but the motto was "Quit Pushing." In light of a lieutenant's life expectancy in Vietnam, our skill level, and our confidence, leadership didn't seem so attractive at that moment.

Jesus also faced a hostile environment. But unlike us, He never questioned His ability as a leader. He lived a perfect, sinless life of obedience to His Father. He modeled how to live and then graciously invited us

79

to follow. Recognizing His authority and gracious character is key to becoming His disciple.

COME AND FOLLOW ME

The Gospel of John begins the account of Jesus' life when He was about thirty years old. There are few recorded facts about Jesus before this time. His cousin, John the Baptist, preceded Jesus' first public appearance by proclaiming a message of repentance, baptism, and anticipation of a coming Messiah. One day as John was teaching, he pointed to Jesus and announced, "Look, the Lamb of God, who takes away the sin of the world!" (John 1:29, NIV).

Two days later Jesus prepared to travel north toward a district called Galilee. Wherever He went, He gave the same invitation: "Come and see." John 1:43-49 describes how a small band of followers began to form around Him:

> The next day Jesus decided to go to Galilee. When he got there, he ran across Philip and said, "Come, follow me." (Philip's hometown was Bethsaida, the same as Andrew and Peter.)
>
> Philip went and found Nathanael and told him, "We've found the One Moses wrote of in the Law, the One preached by the prophets. It's *Jesus*, Joseph's son, the one from Nazareth!" Nathanael said, "Nazareth? You've got to be kidding."
>
> But Philip said, "Come, see for yourself."
>
> When Jesus saw him coming he said, "There's a real Israelite, not a false bone in his body."
>
> Nathanael said, "Where did you get that idea? You don't know me."
>
> Jesus answered, "One day, long before Philip called you here, I saw you under the fig tree."
>
> Nathanael exclaimed, "Rabbi! You are the Son of God, the King of Israel!"

Q1. What do you think motivated Philip to contact his friend Nathanael?

Q2. What changed Nathanael's mind about following Jesus?

Q3. What influenced you to become a follower of Jesus?

It was an honor in Jesus' day to be called "teacher" or "rabbi." Many leading teachers had followers or disciples. There were people who followed the teachings of Socrates, Plato, and even Moses. One group of teachers who had a significant following was the Pharisees. The Pharisees were an influential group of religious teachers who were often in conflict with Jesus.

One key difference between Jesus and other teachers (including the Pharisees) was His invitation to follow. While most teachers said, "Follow my teaching," Jesus said, "Follow Me!" Jesus invited people to come and see who He was. It was an invitation to become personally connected with Him and to share a dynamic experience of friendship and comradeship. In the context of that relationship, Jesus taught truth to His followers. But the primary focus was on following Him.

Chapters 5–7 in the Gospel of Matthew are commonly referred to as the Sermon on the Mount. Jesus described the Kingdom of God to a crowd of disciples as they gathered on a hillside. Matthew 7:28-29 depicts the crowd's reaction to Jesus' teaching: "When Jesus concluded his address, the crowd burst into applause. They had never heard teaching like this. It was apparent that he was living everything he was saying—quite a contrast to their religion teachers! This was the best teaching they had ever heard."

Q4. **How might Jesus' teaching have been different from anything the crowd had heard before? Why do you think the crowd responded so enthusiastically to it?**

Those who continued to follow Jesus were changed. They took on His beliefs, values, and character. Peter and John were two of the more notable disciples who began to speak boldly about their belief in Jesus following His resurrection and ascension into heaven. Their message was often unpopular with the authorities. On one occasion, Peter and John were arrested after healing a lame beggar in Jesus' name. Read what happened next in Acts 4:5-13:

> The next day a meeting was called in Jerusalem. The rulers, religious leaders, religion scholars, Annas the Chief Priest, Caiaphas, John, Alexander—everybody who was anybody was there. They stood Peter and John in the middle of the room and grilled them: "Who put you in charge here? What business do you have doing this?"
>
> With that, Peter, full of the Holy Spirit, let loose: "Rulers and leaders of the people, if we have been brought to trial today for helping a sick man, put under investigation regarding this healing, I'll be completely frank with you—we have nothing to hide. By the name of Jesus Christ of Nazareth, the One you killed on a cross, the One God raised from the dead, by means of his name this man stands before you healthy and whole. Jesus is 'the stone you masons threw out, which is now the cornerstone.' Salvation comes no other way; no other name has been or will be given to us by which we can be saved, only this one."

They couldn't take their eyes off them—Peter and John standing there so confident, so sure of themselves! Their fascination deepened when they realized these two were laymen with no training in Scripture or formal education. They recognized them as companions of Jesus.

Q5.   What is significant about the fact that Peter spoke so boldly about Jesus in front of the authorities? What were Peter's main points?

Q6.   What did the authorities recognize about these early followers?

In spite of threats made by the religious authorities, Peter and John continued to teach about Christ. They were willing to follow Him regardless of the consequences.

COME AND REST

In Matthew 11:25-30, Jesus invited the people to come and see—to observe His life and be changed to be like Him. He also invited them to come and rest—to find the inner peace of mind and spirit that comes from a close relationship with Him.

Abruptly Jesus broke into prayer: "Thank you, Father, Lord of heaven and earth. You've concealed your ways from sophisticates and know-it-alls, but spelled them out clearly to ordinary people. Yes, Father, that's the way you like to work."

Jesus resumed talking to the people, but now tenderly. "The Father has given me all these things to do and say. This is a unique Father-Son operation, coming out of Father and Son intimacies and knowledge. No one knows the Son the way the Father does, nor the Father the way the Son does. But I'm not keeping it to myself; I'm ready to go over it line by line with anyone willing to listen.

"Are you tired? Worn out? Burned out on religion? Come to me. Get away with me and you'll recover your life. I'll show you how to take a real rest. Walk with me and work with me—watch how I do it. Learn the unforced rhythms of grace. I won't lay anything heavy or ill-fitting on you. Keep company with me and you'll learn to live freely and lightly."

Q7. How did Jesus describe the people He invites to come to Him?

Q8. What did Jesus say He will do if we follow Him?

Jesus worked as a carpenter until He was thirty years old. It is likely He would have learned to make a yoke for oxen. In His teaching, Jesus used the metaphor of a yoke to illustrate what it meant to follow Him. The picture was common in His day, though it may be strange to most of us. In Christ's culture, a team of oxen—often two harnessed together by a double yoke—did most of the hard agricultural work. One of the oxen was usually experienced at the task, while the other was learning "on the job."

In the same way, when we become "yoked" with Jesus, He takes the load of our burdens, and we learn to keep in step with Him. As we go in His direction at His speed, we "learn to live freely and lightly."

COME AND LEARN

The terms *follower* and *disciple* are used synonymously in the Bible. The root meaning of the word *disciple* is "learner." When Jesus invites us to follow Him, He is asking us to learn. As we follow Christ, we discover more about who He is and where He is going. This type of discovery is more than knowing facts—it's learning about life through experience.

Two of Jesus' friends, Mary and Martha, had traveled with Him and welcomed Him and His disciples into their home. The following story in Luke 10:38-42 tells about one of the visits Jesus made.

> As they continued their travel, Jesus entered a village. A woman by the name of Martha welcomed him and made him feel quite at home. She had a sister, Mary, who sat before the Master, hanging on every word he said. But Martha was pulled away by all she had to do in the kitchen. Later, she stepped in, interrupting them. "Master, don't you care that my sister has abandoned the kitchen to me? Tell her to lend me a hand."
>
> The Master said, "Martha, dear Martha, you're fussing far too much and getting yourself worked up over nothing. One thing only is essential, and Mary has chosen it—it's the main course, and won't be taken from her."

Q9.   What are the notable differences between Mary and Martha?

Q10.   What is the "main course" Jesus referred to? Why is that the most important thing?

SUMMARY

Just as He did in His earthly ministry, Jesus calls us today to be His followers. He wants us to "come and see" and get to know Him. He calls us to rest from our burdens and to be diligent about learning from Him. When we follow Him, we become like Him.

PRAYER

Thank You, Lord, that You are a leader who not only points out the way to walk but also invites me to come with You on the journey. Thank You that You entered our world for this very purpose. Lord, You know I am prone to be independent. Please help me to stay close to You and Your teaching and not to go off on my own.

HIS BRANCH

We are dependent on Christ as a branch is on a tree.
He is the source through which we receive the essentials of life.
Through us, fruit is produced that reflects and honors Him.

*I am the vine; you are the branches. If you remain in me and I in you,
you will bear much fruit; apart from me you can do nothing.*

JOHN 15:5, NIV

I (MARY) GREW UP in Michigan and loved driving through the country enjoying the beautiful fruit orchards. The hillsides were also dotted with vineyards, but I did not find vineyards very attractive. For most of the year, they looked like rows of stubby sticks. Gnarled vines grew three or four feet out of the ground and were topped by small branches that required the support of a fence. There was little foliage to add beauty. They looked instead like stumps with long, gangly arms.

I have since learned how difficult it is to produce good fruit from those gangly vines and branches. It takes the care of a skilled gardener. The grape branches tend to grow thick and heavy with foliage, often falling to the ground, where the leaves become covered with dirt. Without intervention, these leaves and branches would be susceptible to mildew and rot. The gardener must lift up these branches, wash them off, and attach them to the supporting fence. Off the ground and exposed to the sunlight, the branches can produce healthy fruit.

The gardener must also prune the vines of extra foliage that blocks the sunshine needed to produce healthy grapes, which is why the vines look so bare for much of the year. The gardener must choose between beautiful-looking vines and succulent grapes.

THE VITAL CONNECTION

In John 15:1-8, Jesus used the picture of the grapevine to teach about our relationship with Him. The people in His culture were familiar with vineyards and could understand the parallels immediately. It may take us a bit more work.

This teaching took place during the final days before Jesus was crucified. In the previous chapter, Jesus and His disciples gathered in the upper room of a home in Jerusalem. There they celebrated the Passover (an Old Testament celebration of the Israelites' deliverance from Egypt).

During the evening, Jesus told them again of His upcoming death. It was a sad and confusing time for the disciples. They had come to believe that Jesus was the promised Messiah, but they were still confused about His mission. It didn't matter that Jesus had repeatedly told them He would die and rise again; they still did not understand.

That evening, Jesus led the disciples out of the city to a garden called Gethsemane. As they walked up the hillside, they passed through vineyards. It was a perfect opportunity for Jesus to use this familiar metaphor to teach them. He explained,

> I am the true vine, and my Father is the gardener. He cuts off every branch in me that bears no fruit, while every branch that does bear fruit he prunes so that it will be even more fruitful. You are already clean because of the word I have spoken to you. Remain in me, as I also remain in you. No branch can bear fruit by itself; it must

remain in the vine. Neither can you bear fruit unless you remain in me.

I am the vine; you are the branches. If you remain in me and I in you, you will bear much fruit; apart from me you can do nothing. If you do not remain in me, you are like a branch that is thrown away and withers; such branches are picked up, thrown into the fire and burned. If you remain in me and my words remain in you, ask whatever you wish, and it will be done for you. This is to my Father's glory, that you bear much fruit, showing yourselves to be my disciples.

As the Father has loved me, so have I loved you. Now remain in my love. If you keep my commands, you will remain in my love, just as I have kept my Father's commands and remain in his love. I have told you this so that my joy may be in you and that your joy may be complete.

JOHN 15:1-11, NIV

Q1. In nature, what does the vine do for the branch, and what does the branch do for the vine?

Q2. What was Jesus saying about us in this passage? What does this passage say about our relationship with Him?

Q3. In this metaphor, our heavenly Father is called the gardener. What do these verses say is His goal?

The term *fruit* in the Bible can refer to actual food as well as to good works or godly character. Galatians 5:22-23 lists the fruit of the Holy Spirit (godly character) that results as we abide in the vine: "But when the Holy Spirit controls our lives he will produce this kind of fruit in us: love, joy, peace, patience, kindness, goodness, faithfulness, gentleness and self-control" (TLB). Jesus taught that fruitfulness is not achievable on our own.

Q4. According to John 15:5, what is required for fruitfulness? How do we practically fulfill this requirement?

In John 15:7, Jesus related the idea of abiding (remaining) in Him with the similar idea of God's Word abiding in us. The idea of abiding or remaining is more than gathering information. It involves understanding, personalization, and consistency. Getting God's Word into our minds and hearts is part of the abiding process. When we let God speak to us through His Word and we speak to Him through prayer, we develop an abiding relationship. This two-way conversation is not something reserved only for times of crisis but should be a normal pattern of our daily lives.

Q5. According to the following Scripture passages, what are the results of remaining vitally connected to (or abiding in) Jesus?

- John 15:7

- John 15:8

• John 15:11

THE PROPER CARE

God, our spiritual gardener, helps us be fruitful in two ways: by cleansing and by pruning. Just as a gardener lifts up branches that are not bearing fruit and cleans them, God lifts us up and gives us a chance to bear fruit. He also prunes branches that are bearing fruit so they can become more fruitful.

In 1 John 1:9, John further explained how God cleanses or lifts us up: "If we confess our sins, he is faithful and just and will forgive us our sins and purify us from all unrighteousness" (NIV).

Q6. What is our role in the cleansing process? What is God's role?

When the Bible tells us to confess our sins, it means we are to admit that what we did (or didn't do) was wrong and to change direction and live God's way. Because of Jesus' sacrifice—the shedding of His blood on the cross—our sin is no longer a barrier to our union with God. We have been adopted into His family and made rightful heirs or children. The Bible tells us, "For Christ also suffered once for sins, the righteous for the unrighteous, to bring you to God" (1 Peter 3:18, NIV).

While no longer a barrier, sin *does* affect your relationship with God. When a child disobeys his parents, there is a sense of estrangement that must be removed through confession and reconciliation. So, too, when we disobey God, we lose the intimacy of our relationship. Like grape leaves that have fallen into the dirt, we need to be picked up, cleansed, and refocused on the light.

When I (Ron) was younger, my father had a variety of fruit trees that he eagerly pruned each fall. Most of the time the pruning helped promote future growth, but sometimes too much pruning actually caused harm. We eagerly waited for spring to see which trees had survived the fall pruning.

Even expert gardeners sometimes prune too much. But our Father is the perfect pruner. He never takes off too much or leaves too little. When our lives become cluttered, consuming valuable resources and limiting the spiritual fruit in our lives, God gets out the pruning shears.

Q7. How does God, our heavenly gardener, prune us?

Q8. Read the following passage and identify the things God wants to prune from our lives.

> Don't love the world's ways. Don't love the world's goods. Love of the world squeezes out love for the Father. Practically everything that goes on in the world—wanting your own way, wanting everything for yourself, wanting to appear important—has nothing to do with the Father. It just isolates you from him.
>
> 1 JOHN 2:15-16

Q9. How have you experienced God's pruning in your life?

Right or wrong one branch will attach to another
a branch growing in the wrong direction
eating may need to be pruned

THE DELIGHTFUL CONCLUSION

In John 15:12-16, Jesus wrapped up the vine-and-branch metaphor. He concluded with these words:

> This is my command: Love one another the way I loved you. This is the very best way to love. Put your life on the line for your friends. You are my friends when you do the things I command you. I'm no longer calling you servants because servants don't understand what their master is thinking and planning. No, I've named you friends because I've let you in on everything I've heard from the Father.
>
> You didn't choose me, remember; I chose you, and put you in the world to bear fruit, fruit that won't spoil. As fruit bearers, whatever you ask the Father in relation to me, he gives you.

Q10.   What did Jesus promise in the passage above?

As we abide in Christ, we learn to love Him. What does this love look like? It looks like willing obedience to live as He directs. The relationship is not one of slave to master but of friend to friend. Joy, lasting fruitfulness, and divine friendship are the amazing results of abiding in Christ.

SUMMARY

We are branches in God's vineyard and have been given the exciting purpose of bearing fruit for Him. Fruitfulness comes as we abide in Jesus and experience the loving touch of our Father, the gardener. Time spent reading and meditating on God's Word helps us abide in Christ. His Word can cleanse our hearts, direct our paths, and change our perspectives.

PRAYER

Lord, thank You so much for the times You've lifted me up and cleansed me. Thank You for helping me remain connected to You. I want to bear fruit for You. Help me accept the necessary pruning to become all You want me to be.

HIS DWELLING PLACE

Through the Holy Spirit, God takes up residence in our lives. His presence is our source of divine power. The Holy Spirit not only helps us understand what to do but also enables us to actually do it.

You realize, don't you, that you are the temple of God,
and God himself is present in you?

1 CORINTHIANS 3:16

WHAT A JOY IT WAS TO FULFILL A DREAM! After seventeen years of living in homes built by others, we had the opportunity to design and build our own. This was going to be the place our kids would remember fondly for years. It would be the place where memories were made and friendships were forged. It would likely be the first and last time we would create a home from the ground up—a home that was uniquely "us."

We borrowed from the best of all we had seen and experienced, put it into a blueprint, and started to build. Every room had a purpose; every window and door was carefully planned to reflect who we were. Working with a general contractor, we built what we could and hired others to do what we couldn't. We were involved with every phase, every crew, and every obstacle. Day by day the house took shape. The final inspection came as the last crew left.

And we moved in.

The house may have taken only four months to build, but it has taken years for it to feel like home. Now the rooms are filled with more than furniture. They are filled with memories of laughter, tears, anxiety, and celebration. The kids have since grown up and moved on, and though we may live in other places in the future, we're certain no other place will be like this one.

One of the most exciting truths about your new life in Christ is the reality that God's Spirit actually takes up residence in your life to connect, guide, and comfort you in the deepest part of your soul. Prior to the coming of the Holy Spirit, God's Spirit was at work in the world but had never permanently "indwelt" (or moved into) His people. This was made possible only by the death and resurrection of Christ. That event opened the door to a whole new way of relating to God.

One of the promises God made to His people throughout biblical history was that He would be with them. God said to Joshua as he prepared to lead Israel into the Promised Land, "Be strong and courageous, for . . . I myself will be with you" (Deuteronomy 31:23, NIV). Jesus said to His first disciples just before He returned to heaven after His resurrection, "I am with you always, even to the end of the age" (Matthew 28:20, NLT). God's presence in the lives of His children is not just theoretical; it is literal!

As the early church began to develop and the message of the gospel spread, the presence of the Holy Spirit in individual believers' lives was often marked by unique events and miracles. As we read their stories (primarily in the book of Acts), we see how important it is to understand this truth of God's presence within us.

The Scripture writers sometimes talked about God or Christ or the Holy Spirit being in us. Each is an expression of the same truth. The apostle John built on this truth in a word picture we can easily relate to: "Behold, I stand at the door and knock; if anyone hears My voice and opens the door, I will come in to him and will dine with him, and he with Me" (Revelation 3:20, NASB).

Christ seeks fellowship at the door of your soul. He knocks and waits for you to open the door and give Him access. When you do, He promises to enter and have close personal fellowship with you. The choice, however, is yours. His presence in you does not mean you will automatically give Him access to all that you are. Learning to give God access to the various rooms in your heart is the journey of a lifetime.

Robert Munger, in his timeless book *My Heart—Christ's Home*, describes the experience this way:

> One evening that I shall never forget, I invited him into my
> heart. What an entrance he made! It was not a spectacular,
> emotional thing, but very real. It was at the very center of
> my life. He came into the darkness of my heart and turned
> on the light. He built a fire in the cold hearth and banished
> the chill. He started music where there had been stillness
> and he filled the emptiness with his own loving, wonderful
> fellowship. I have never regretted opening the door to Christ
> and I never will—not into eternity![1]

GOD'S PRESENCE IN US

Jesus told His early followers that He would leave them and yet would be present with them. How could this be? The answer is found in the coming of the Holy Spirit (the third person of the Trinity), which is recorded in the book of Acts and described as the Day of Pentecost.

Paul affirmed in 1 Corinthians 6:19-20 that the Holy Spirit dwells within believers by referring to them as the temple of God:

> Didn't you realize that your body is a sacred place, the place of the
> Holy Spirit? Don't you see that you can't live however you please,

squandering what God paid such a high price for? The physical part of you is not some piece of property belonging to the spiritual part of you. God owns the whole works. So let people see God in and through your body.

The Temple in the Old Testament was the place where God "lived." If people wanted to get close to God, they went to the Temple. Since Christ's resurrection, God no longer dwells in a building but in the lives of His people. This reality has a tremendous impact on who we are and what we are called to do.

Jesus described the coming role of the Holy Spirit to His early followers:

If you love me, show it by doing what I've told you. I will talk to the Father, and he'll provide you another Friend so that you will always have someone with you. This Friend is the Spirit of Truth. The godless world can't take him in because it doesn't have eyes to see him, doesn't know what to look for. But you know him already because he has been staying with you, and will even be *in* you!

I will not leave you orphaned. I'm coming back. In just a little while the world will no longer see me, but you're going to see me because I am alive and you're about to come alive. At that moment you will know absolutely that I'm in my Father, and you're in me, and I'm in you.

The person who knows my commandments and keeps them, that's who loves me. And the person who loves me will be loved by my Father, and I will love him and make myself plain to him. . . .

I'm telling you these things while I'm still living with you. The Friend, the Holy Spirit whom the Father will send at my request, will make everything plain to you. He will remind you of all the things I have told you.

JOHN 14:15-21, 25-26

Q1. In this passage, how is the Holy Spirit described?

Q2. What will the Holy Spirit do as He lives within each believer?

Q3. What happens when we respond to the Holy Spirit through obedience?

GOD'S WORK FOR US

The Holy Spirit is often referred to as our Counselor, Helper, or Comforter. He leads us, teaches us truth, and helps us apply it. In John 16:5-15, Jesus explained what would happen after His resurrection:

Now I am on my way to the One who sent me. Not one of you has asked, "Where are you going?" Instead, the longer I've talked, the sadder you've become. So let me say it again, this truth: It's better for you that I leave. If I don't leave, the Friend won't come. But if I go, I'll send him to you.

When he comes, he'll expose the error of the godless world's view of sin, righteousness, and judgment: He'll show them that their refusal to believe in me is their basic sin; that righteousness comes from above, where I am with the Father, out of their sight and control; that judgment takes place as the ruler of this godless world is brought to trial and convicted.

I still have many things to tell you, but you can't handle them now. But when the Friend comes, the Spirit of the Truth, he will take you by the hand and guide you into all the truth there is. He won't draw attention to himself, but will make sense out of what is about to happen and, indeed, out of all that I have done and said. He will honor me; he will take from me and deliver it to you. Everything the Father has is also mine. That is why I've said, "He takes from me and delivers to you."

Q4. Why did Jesus say, "It's better for you that I leave"?

Q5. In this passage, what did Jesus say the Holy Spirit will do?

The Holy Spirit helps us by guiding and comforting and also by bringing divine power to our lives. Jesus told His disciples, "You will receive power when the Holy Spirit comes on you; and you will be my witnesses in Jerusalem, and in all Judea and Samaria, and to the ends of the earth" (Acts 1:8, NIV).

Living the Christian life is possible only through the power of God and His Spirit. The life God has designed us for and calls us to is so awesome, so different from what we have known, that we can't do it on our own. His indwelling Spirit is our resource for divine power. We must learn to rely on Him.

GOD'S EXPECTATION OF US

Because we are children of God, the Holy Spirit dwells within us and is ready to guide, comfort, and empower us. But He invites our cooperation.

Q6. **In the Scripture passages that follow, circle our role in cooperating with God's Spirit.**

Be cheerful no matter what; pray all the time; thank God no matter what happens. This is the way God wants you who belong to Christ Jesus to live.

Don't suppress the Spirit, and don't stifle those who have a word from the Master. On the other hand, don't be gullible. Check out everything, and keep only what's good. Throw out anything tainted with evil.

1 THESSALONIANS 5:16-22

Don't grieve God. Don't break his heart. His Holy Spirit, moving and breathing in you, is the most intimate part of your life, making you fit for himself. Don't take such a gift for granted.

Make a clean break with all cutting, backbiting, profane talk. Be gentle with one another, sensitive. Forgive one another as quickly and thoroughly as God in Christ forgave you.

EPHESIANS 4:30-32

Since, then, we do not have the excuse of ignorance, everything— and I do mean everything—connected with that old way of life has to go. It's rotten through and through. Get rid of it! And then take on an entirely new way of life—a God-fashioned life, a life renewed from the inside and working itself into your conduct as God accurately reproduces his character in you.

EPHESIANS 4:22-24

You groped your way through that murk once, but no longer. You're out in the open now. The bright light of Christ makes your way plain. So no more stumbling around. Get on with it!

EPHESIANS 5:8

Q7. Summarize what we need to do to cooperate with the Holy Spirit.

Paul said in Philippians 2:13, "God is working in you, giving you the desire and the power to do what pleases him" (NLT). His presence with us is assurance that we are never alone. Nothing can separate us from the love of God because His Spirit takes up residence in our lives. The journey we are on requires us to learn how to cooperate with His Spirit. But God reminds us that whenever He requires us to do something, He also gives us the power to do it.

SUMMARY

We are the dwelling place of God. Through His Spirit, God is present in this world in the life of each believer. His Spirit guides, comforts, instructs, and empowers us. We walk in step with His Spirit through the Word of God and prayer. As we grow in our relationship with Christ, we will learn more about how the Holy Spirit works.

PRAYER

I am so grateful for the incredible truth that You live in me. I want to be a worthy dwelling place. Help me give You the freedom to clean up the junk that has accumulated in my life. Thank You for the presence and power of the Holy Spirit living in me. Thank You that the Holy Spirit guides and comforts me. Help me fully cooperate with the Holy Spirit by following His leading.

SUMMARY

USE THE FOLLOWING CHART to review the lessons you have just completed. You may want to show someone else what you have been learning about your journey with Christ.

LESSON	KEY VERSE	GOD IS MY ...	MY RESPONSE IS TO ...	THIS RESULTS IN ...
His Workmanship	Isaiah 64:8	Sovereign Creator	Recognize and accept my unique design and value	Contentment and hope
His Sheep	John 10:11	Good Shepherd	Know, listen to, and follow His voice	Freedom from anxiety
His Child	John 1:12	Heavenly Father	Trust in His goodness and wisdom	A sense of belonging and security
His Follower	Matthew 4:19	Gracious Leader	Learn to respond to His directions	New ways of thinking and living
His Branch	John 15:5	Resourceful Vine	Abide in Christ consistently through His Word	Lasting fruitfulness in and through my life
His Dwelling Place	1 Corinthians 3:16	Divine Presence	Cooperate with His Spirit within me	The touch of God's power to live beyond my own means

ONE OF THE GREAT MEMORIES I (Ron) have from my childhood is a canoe trip I took with my dad and cousin into the Boundary Waters of Canada. We had done some basic family camping before, but this was the "big one." This was like going out with Lewis and Clark.

Wisely, my dad decided to break with the tradition of outfitting ourselves with only what we had or could borrow. Instead, he hired an outfitter to put together the equipment and supplies for our backwoods adventure. It was expensive and seemed extravagant in light of my dad's frugal mind-set, but he reasoned, "It's a once-in-a-lifetime trip, so maybe it's better to be safe than sorry."

We arrived at the outfitter's northern outpost midafternoon. It was warm and sunny, and my excitement was indescribable. The canoes were already loaded on the truck. We threw in the four large duffel bags of supplies that were provided for us and drove off with the outfitter to our launch point.

This was to be a seven-day round-trip through the chain of lakes that make up the Minnesota and Canadian Boundary Waters, and we would be guided by only a map, a compass, and our courage. The outfitter left us with the parting words "I'll be back in seven days to pick you up. Everything you need is in those duffel bags." Our last contact with civilization drove away down the dusty gravel road. We pushed off into the unknown. As far as we knew, we would not see another human being for seven days.

The content of those duffel bags was the last thing on my mind as we glided across the clear, azure blue water in search of our first portage. Those bags at that moment were simply cushions against the aluminum frame of the canoe. Who had time to consider them? We were three guys living on the wild side!

It was during our first portage that I became curious about their contents. Two hundred yards of dragging the bags uphill over rocks as we hiked made me wonder what made them so heavy. Did we really need it all? Had they given us supplies for a month instead of seven days? What if we hid one of the bags in a tree and picked it up on our return trip? But, no. Dad, convinced that everything we had was essential, made sure each item was carefully repacked as we completed each subsequent portage.

I can't remember which came first, the darkness or the rain, but both were intimidating. Looking for a suitable campsite at night in a thunderstorm made even my dad a little nervous. We eventually came upon a small island that, compared to struggling against the wind and whitecaps, seemed like a reasonable choice. Soaked, cold, and hungry, we unpacked the canoes and dragged the equipment to a clearing on a rocky ledge.

"I wonder if they packed a tent?" I remember asking. "I'm sure they did," my dad replied. "I just hope we can figure out how to put it up!" I hadn't even thought of that. If there *were* instructions, the middle of the night in the middle of a lake in the middle of a storm was not a good time to start reading them!

Eventually we found, unpacked, and set up the tent. Three wet, hungry, and tired bodies crawled into the relative safety of our shelter held down from the gusting wind by a hasty pile of stones in lieu of tent stakes, which we discovered didn't work well on solid rock.

With our supplies safely stored and under the illumination of a small flashlight, we began to explore the contents of our four duffel bags. We looked like three raccoons foraging for food in a picnic basket. We discovered food, matches, fuel, a knife, a hatchet, and rain ponchos. It was a little late for the ponchos, but we agreed we'd use them in the next storm. Other items were carefully noted, dried, and repacked for later use.

Seven days later we met our outfitter at the prearranged pickup point and headed back to civilization. Everything we needed during our journey had been in those duffel bags. Evidently the one who packed our supplies had made the trip before. As it turned out, there was no extra weight in the bags.

In a similar way, Christ has made the journey before us and has packed our faith journey's duffel bags. Everything we need for our adventure with Him is included. In the following lessons, we'll take a brief look into those duffel bags at some of the essential supplies we'll need for this incredible journey called life.

Knowing what's available can make setting up camp less threatening. But if you don't understand it all right now, that's okay. Your guide has not only packed your bags, but He is also traveling with you. Christ is your outfitter *and* guide. He has been down the road before, and nothing you encounter will be a surprise to Him.

In this final section we will look at our resources of

- Faith
- The Word
- Prayer
- The Holy Spirit
- Grace
- Community

FAITH

Faith is essential to our journey with Christ. It is the currency of God's Kingdom. It takes us every place we need to go. Faith allows us to see the invisible reality of God's Kingdom, it is the means by which we relate to God, and it inspires us to face the unknown with certainty.

Trust in the LORD with all your heart
and lean not on your own understanding;
in all your ways submit to him,
and he will make your paths straight.

PROVERBS 3:5-6, NIV

FOLLOWING THE RUSSIAN LAUNCH of the orbiting unmanned satellite Sputnik 1 in the late 1950s, space interest reached an all-time high. America was playing catch-up but eventually made plans to place men on the moon. It was in that environment that I (Ron) began my undergraduate study in aerospace engineering.

In one of our courses, we were given an assignment to design a vehicle that astronauts could use to explore the surface of the moon. Because we had no firsthand knowledge of the composition of the moon's surface (we did know it wasn't made of cheese), the vehicle needed to be able to handle any kind of surface and terrain. What we came up with was akin to an early prototype of an all-terrain vehicle (ATV).

ATVs today are only remotely similar to our class project or even to the actual moon explorer. But they serve the same purpose. Mary and I rode an ATV over a twelve-thousand-foot mountain pass in Colorado. On our journey we encountered every kind of terrain possible—water, rocks, dirt, sand, and snow. Part of the adventure was learning to trust the capability of our vehicle. As we conquered each obstacle, we grew more confident for the next.

Our life with Christ requires faith from beginning to end. It is our vehicle for traveling on this incredible journey. It is essential and is not something we outgrow. The more we understand about faith, the more we will come to rely on its power for daily living.

FAITH AND REALITY

The word *faith*, like so many words in our culture, can have many meanings. It's often used to convey optimism. We say to someone who is facing the unknown, "Just have faith." Sometimes it refers to a whole body of religious teaching, such as "They were strong in their faith."

When the Bible uses the term *faith*, it is referring to a trust in something *real yet unseen* that inspires action in the direction of that belief. The book of Hebrews explains it well: "The fundamental fact of existence is that this trust in God, this faith, is the firm foundation under everything that makes life worth living. It's our handle on what we can't see" (11:1).

Q1. What does this passage say about faith?

Dreams (vs) faith

Biblical faith is more than optimism. Biblical faith is not a dream or pretending. Dreams deal with what we hope will happen. Faith deals with what is happening but is simply not visible or seen . . . yet. It is more than a set of religious beliefs; it is a confident trust built on God, His character, and His Word.

FAITH AND GOD

If you told someone, "Trust me," what you'd really be saying is "You can count on me to keep my promise." However, though you may have good intentions, you might lack the ability or opportunity to do what you promised. Faith must have a reliable object or source for trust.

The *Peanuts* comic strip featured a recurring scenario in which Lucy would hold a football for Charlie Brown to kick. In each cartoon Lucy talked Charlie into trusting her to hold the ball. In each cartoon she pulled it away at the last minute. And in each cartoon Charlie Brown ended up on his backside, vowing never to trust her again. But the optimistic Charlie put his faith in Lucy time after time.

Fortunately, biblical faith doesn't rely on a "Lucy" as its foundation. Biblical faith is always based on God and His Word. Look at this statement from Hebrews 11:6: "Without faith it is impossible to please God, because anyone who comes to him must believe that he exists and that he rewards those who earnestly seek him" (NIV).

Q2. What does this passage tell us is essential in order for us to please God?

Q3. Why is trust in God necessary to please Him?

If our faith is not based on God's Word or His character, it may be optimism or positive thinking—but it is not biblical faith. When God speaks, we can count on it. God has not only the desire but also the ability to keep His word. When God makes a promise, He wants us to believe it and act in light of it.

Ultimately our faith in God comes down to our trust in His character.

The more we understand and experience God in our lives, the greater our confidence becomes. As we see God keep His promises, our trust in His character grows. Our spiritual lives mature as we "taste and see that the Lord is good" and realize that "blessed is the man who takes refuge in him" (Psalm 34:8, NIV).

When Charlton Heston was filming the classic movie *Ben-Hur*, he did most of his own stunts, including the famous and dangerous chariot race. Legend has it that at the conclusion of his training and practice, Heston expressed to the trainer his concern that in the actual filming he might not be good enough to win the race. The trainer replied that if Heston would make sure he stayed in the chariot, the trainer would make sure he won. Faith is putting trust or confidence in someone other than ourselves who has the ability to do all that he says he'll do.

FAITH AND ACTION

Real faith always involves a response; it prompts us to move in the direction of our trust. When we have faith in God, we trust Him to do what He says He'll do, and we take steps of action in accordance with that belief. We may not always feel safe as we take these steps of faith, but our feelings are often a poor indicator of truth. It's true that faith does involve risk, particularly because we are reaching beyond our own resources and ability for what God has promised. But this is not a static amount of risk. In fact, our willingness to risk increases as our understanding of God grows.

Jesus often taught about faith during His ministry. His initial followers frequently struggled to understand this concept. During one of Jesus' teaching sessions, two very different people came to Him, and their actions helped clarify what faith is. Read the story of Jairus and the woman in this passage from Luke and look for answers to the questions that follow.

On his return, Jesus was welcomed by a crowd. They were all there expecting him. A man came up, Jairus by name. He was president of the meeting place. He fell at Jesus' feet and begged him to come to his home because his twelve-year-old daughter, his only child, was dying. Jesus went with him, making his way through the pushing, jostling crowd.

In the crowd that day there was a woman who for twelve years had been afflicted with hemorrhages. She had spent every penny she had on doctors but not one had been able to help her. She slipped in from behind and touched the edge of Jesus' robe. At that very moment her hemorrhaging stopped. Jesus said, "Who touched me?"

When no one stepped forward, Peter said, "But Master, we've got crowds of people on our hands. Dozens have touched you."

Jesus insisted, "Someone touched me. I felt power discharging from me."

When the woman realized that she couldn't remain hidden, she knelt trembling before him. In front of all the people, she blurted out her story—why she touched him and how at that same moment she was healed.

Jesus said, "Daughter, you took a risk trusting me, and now you're healed and whole. Live well, live blessed!"

While he was still talking, someone from the leader's [Jairus's] house came up and told him, "Your daughter died. No need now to bother the Teacher."

Jesus overheard and said, "Don't be upset. Just trust me and everything will be all right." Going into the house, he wouldn't let anyone enter with him except Peter, John, James, and the child's parents.

Everyone was crying and carrying on over her. Jesus said, "Don't cry. She didn't die; she's sleeping." They laughed at him. They knew she was dead.

Then Jesus, gripping her hand, called, "My dear child, get up."
She was up in an instant, up and breathing again! He told them to
give her something to eat. Her parents were ecstatic, but Jesus
warned them to keep quiet. "Don't tell a soul what happened in
this room."

LUKE 8:40-56

Q4. How did Jairus and the woman each demonstrate faith?

Q5. What beliefs prompted their actions?

Q6. What risks did each person take?

Q7. Why do you think Jesus exposed the woman's faith publicly?

Q8. How did Jesus describe unseen reality?

One of the unique aspects of our walk with Christ is that faith makes us
all equal. Background, status, position, and natural abilities are irrelevant
to God. The two people in the story you just read had vastly different
lifestyles. Yet they both related to Jesus personally through faith. Our
common ground in Christ is faith.

Faith also allows us to live in unseen reality. Electricity is an unseen reality that we now take for granted—it's a power that remains invisible until we take the action of plugging into it. Jairus and the woman in the story had to "plug in" to Christ and His power as well.

Hebrews 11:6 makes it clear that having faith is essential to pleasing God. God always responds to faith in Him. Though we begin our walk with Christ by faith, too often we try to continue that relationship on the basis of merit. We think erroneously that while faith was adequate to get us started, it's not enough to keep God's favor. Don't make this mistake. From beginning to end, the journey with Christ is by faith.

Faith brings miraculous peace to the stormy seasons of life. Your walk with Christ won't eliminate the tensions and pain of life in a broken world, but you can be at peace even if your world is in chaos. Sometimes God stills the storms, and other times He carries us through them.

Hebrews 11:13-31 describes some of the biblical heroes of faith who, despite difficult circumstances in life, maintained their faith in God and found peace.

Each one of these people of faith died not yet having in hand what was promised, but still believing. How did they do it? They saw it way off in the distance, waved their greeting, and accepted the fact that they were transients in this world. People who live this way make it plain that they are looking for their true home. If they were homesick for the old country, they could have gone back any time they wanted. But they were after a far better country than that— *heaven* country. You can see why God is so proud of them, and has a City waiting for them.

By faith, Abraham, at the time of testing, offered Isaac back to God. Acting in faith, he was as ready to return the promised son, his only son, as he had been to receive him—and this after he had already been told, "Your descendants shall come from Isaac." Abraham figured that if God wanted to, he could raise the dead.

In a sense, that's what happened when he received Isaac back, alive from off the altar.

By an act of faith, Isaac reached into the future as he blessed Jacob and Esau.

By an act of faith, Jacob on his deathbed blessed each of Joseph's sons in turn, blessing them with God's blessing, not his own—as he bowed worshipfully upon his staff.

By an act of faith, Joseph, while dying, prophesied the exodus of Israel, and made arrangements for his own burial.

By an act of faith, Moses' parents hid him away for three months after his birth. They saw the child's beauty, and they braved the king's decree.

By faith, Moses, when grown, refused the privileges of the Egyptian royal house. He chose a hard life with God's people rather than an opportunistic soft life of sin with the oppressors. He valued suffering in the Messiah's camp far greater than Egyptian wealth because he was looking ahead, anticipating the payoff. By an act of faith, he turned his heel on Egypt, indifferent to the king's blind rage. He had his eye on the One no eye can see, and kept right on going. By an act of faith, he kept the Passover Feast and sprinkled Passover blood on each house so that the destroyer of the firstborn wouldn't touch them.

By an act of faith, Israel walked through the Red Sea on dry ground. The Egyptians tried it and drowned.

By faith, the Israelites marched around the walls of Jericho for seven days, and the walls fell flat.

By an act of faith, Rahab, the Jericho harlot, welcomed the spies and escaped the destruction that came on those who refused to trust God.

Q9. How did each of these people demonstrate faith?

Q10. Which one do you admire the most? Why?

SUMMARY

Faith is not wishful thinking or spiritual optimism. It is belief in the unseen reality that God has promised. Faith is only as sure as the object of the faith. As Christians, our faith is in the unchanging character and Word of God. This kind of faith results in responsive action.

PRAYER

Father, I believe that You are absolutely reliable. I can count on every word You have spoken, every promise You have made. When the future looks uncertain, when my heart begins to fear, or when confusion tries to overwhelm me, I will hold on to You as my rock, my fortress, and my secure foundation.

LESSON 14

THE WORD

The Bible is God's personal Word to us. It is absolutely true and reliable.
It is God's way of revealing Himself to us and serves as a how-to-live manual.
As we understand it, believe it, and apply it to our lives,
we will experience its power and benefits.

I am but a pilgrim here on earth: how I need a map—
and your commands are my chart and guide. I long for your
instructions more than I can tell.

PSALM 119:19-20, TLB

ON SEPTEMBER 11, 1777, George Washington prepared to defend Philadelphia from the British army led by General Howe. Both Washington and Howe were fighting in unfamiliar territory along Brandywine Creek. Washington's plan was not only to defend Philadelphia but also to take the offensive and surround Howe's army. His strategy was based on the location of river crossings along Brandywine Creek as noted on the maps he had been given.

Washington almost met disaster during the night as Howe's army crossed above Washington's right flank at a point called Jeffries Ford. Washington's map showed Jeffries Ford ten miles north of his army's position. In reality it was only two miles north. Washington had a solid strategy, but it was based on inaccurate maps. Only a hasty retreat saved the fragile American army from certain defeat.

Nothing is more critical when traveling in unfamiliar territory than an accurate map. An accurate map not only tells us the best route to our destination, but it also tells us what we can expect to encounter along the way. The Bible is God's road map for our walk with Christ.

The Bible is an amazing book. It is not a novel, although it contains some dramatic stories. It is not an encyclopedia, although it deals with every critical area of life. The Bible, also called Scripture or the Word, is made up of sixty-six books and divided into two major sections referred to as the Old and New Testaments. Forty different writers wrote the Bible over a fifteen-hundred-year period. The authors were kings, prophets, peasants, fishermen, poets, and philosophers. Yet with all this diversity, the Bible carries a common theme and unity throughout. This amazing unity suggests that there was one true Author . . . God Himself.

With regard to history, the Bible continues to be remarkable. The city of Jericho (mentioned in the Old Testament) was part of Israel's story. Undiscovered until 1930, the ruins of Jericho were finally found buried beneath the desert sand at the very location given in the Bible. The walls of the city had fallen outward as the Bible described, rather than inward as would be suggested by an invasion.

There are more than three hundred prophecies (or God-given predictions) referring to Christ, the coming Messiah, in the Old Testament. Written hundreds of years before Christ, all three hundred came true. The mathematical probability that these prophecies would all be fulfilled in one man is staggering and would be impossible apart from the divine authorship of a sovereign God.

God's preservation of the Bible over the past thirty-five hundred years is further remarkable evidence of its divine authorship. Up until 1947, the earliest manuscripts we had of the Bible were from the ninth and tenth centuries AD. Although these handwritten documents encompassed only the first five books of the Bible, they gave incredible verification of the Bible's accuracy as a work of ancient writing.

But in 1947 in a cave near the Dead Sea, manuscripts of every Old Testament book except Esther were found and determined to be from

125 BC. Amazingly preserved, these documents were compared with those written one thousand years later. Very few differences were discovered, and those that were had no impact on the text's meaning. This suggests that God not only gave the words originally but also preserved His words throughout history so that we might have an accurate and authoritative record of His message today.

Q1. Which of the following best describes what you believe the Bible to be?

_____ A book of myths and fables

_____ A book of ancient sacred writings that are no longer relevant

_____ A book with some good, practical advice

_____ A unique book that is from God and is reliably true

_____ Other: *Basic instructions before leaving earth*

Q2. Why (or how) did you develop that view?

THE BIBLE AND TRUTH

The Bible is true not because it rates high in opinion polls or fits current philosophy, but because God said it is true. Read what it says in 2 Peter 1:20-21: "For no prophecy recorded in Scripture was ever thought up by the prophet himself. It was the Holy Spirit within these godly men who gave them true messages from God" (TLB).

The Bible claims that when it speaks on a subject, it speaks truth. Jesus verified that the Old Testament was authentic and true. He quoted Old Testament Scripture frequently and based His ministry on it. He said everything that was promised in the Scriptures would come true. Jesus said, "Sanctify them by the truth; your [God's] word is truth" (John 17:17, NIV).

The Bible has been the focus of great criticism, skepticism, and persecution throughout history. Yet it continues to prove itself true in every generation. It is an anchor in a stormy sea of confusion. The truth of the Bible stands in contrast to the culture of relativism. When other philosophies have come and gone, the Bible will remain. Jesus said, "Heaven and earth will pass away, but my words will never pass away" (Mark 13:31, NIV).

The Bible is the progressive revelation of who God is and how He relates to people. The Bible doesn't tell us everything there is to know about God, but it does tell us enough so that we can relate to Him and live effectively. It is our true source of knowledge about the nature and heart of God. Our natural world may imply certain characteristics of God, but the Bible explains His heart. For example, most people looking at the awesome beauty and complexity of nature would admit that God is powerful and creative. Yet without the Bible, we would never know that God loves people so much that He was willing to leave the timelessness of heaven to live among us as a servant. We can see the power of creation in nature, but we would not see the power of the Cross without the Bible.

David wrote in Psalm 19:7-11 (NIV),

> The law of the LORD is perfect,
>   refreshing the soul.
> The statutes of the LORD are trustworthy,
>   making wise the simple.
> The precepts of the LORD are right,
>   giving joy to the heart.
> The commands of the LORD are radiant,
>   giving light to the eyes.
> The fear of the LORD is pure,
>   enduring forever.
> The decrees of the LORD are firm
>   and all of them are righteous.
> They are more precious than gold,

than much pure gold;
they are sweeter than honey,
than honey from the honeycomb.
By them your servant is warned;
in keeping them there is great reward.

Q3.   How did David describe God's Word?

Q4.   What was David's conclusion about God's Word? How does that compare to your conclusion?

THE BIBLE AND SUCCESS

You can study the Bible like any other book in the library. You may have even tried to read parts of it in the past with mixed results. One unique characteristic of the Bible is that once you begin your faith journey with Christ, it becomes your word from God—a personal letter from your Father. Additionally, Jesus promised that the Holy Spirit would help us to understand it—and not just an academic or historical understanding, but a comprehension of the heart.

The apostle Paul wrote to new believers who had experienced the power of God's personal word, "Now we look back on all this and thank God, an artesian well of thanks! When you got the Message of God we preached, you didn't pass it off as just one more human opinion, but you took it to heart as God's true word to you, which it is, God himself at work in you believers!" (1 Thessalonians 2:13).

For followers of Christ, the Bible is more than an ancient book of stories—it's God's resource for sustaining their lives. I have heard people who recently began their faith walk say this about the Bible:

- "I tried reading the Bible before, but it was dry and boring. Now I read the same thing and it is alive and exciting."
- "I couldn't pick it up before, and now I can't put it down."
- "Before coming to Christ, the Bible was like reading someone else's mail. Now it's like having my own letter from God."

The Bible is God's primary means of speaking to us today. Reading and studying the Bible is how we develop a dialogue with God. God speaks to us through His Word, and we speak to Him through prayer. This two-way communication builds our relationship with Christ into something both personal and dynamic.

The Bible is like a how-to-live manual, a self-help book for life. It addresses not only spiritual issues but also earthly issues such as how to handle money or get along with a spouse. The Bible contains truth for conducting business as well as raising a family.

Paul summarized the importance and practical value of the Bible in his final letter to Timothy: "Every part of Scripture is God-breathed and useful one way or another—showing us truth, exposing our rebellion, correcting our mistakes, training us to live God's way. Through the Word we are put together and shaped up for the tasks God has for us" (2 Timothy 3:16-17).

Q5. Based on this passage, what are four practical uses of the Bible, and how are they different?

There are many good translations of the Bible available today. We encourage you to get an inexpensive paperback version of the whole Bible and make it your own by reading it and marking in it. Highlighting words or phrases that stand out to you as you read is a good way to make the Bible personal.

THE BIBLE AND OBEDIENCE

The Bible was not given to increase our knowledge
but to change our lives.

—D. L. MOODY

Because the Bible was written in the context of real life, it contains facts of history, science, psychology, and geography. At a superficial level, this is valuable information. However, God's intent in giving us His Word was not only to bring us new information but also to give us truth to live by. It is in the understanding, belief, and application of Scripture that we discover its greatest value.

Jesus' most famous and comprehensive "how to live" message is the Sermon on the Mount (recorded in Matthew 5–7). In this talk, Jesus described what it looks like to live as His follower. At the very end of His message, He told this famous story:

> Therefore everyone who hears these words of mine and puts them into practice is like a wise man who built his house on the rock. The rain came down, the streams rose, and the winds blew and beat against that house; yet it did not fall, because it had its foundation on the rock. But everyone who hears these words of mine and does not put them into practice is like a foolish man who built his house on sand. The rain came down, the streams rose, and the winds blew and beat against that house, and it fell with a great crash.
> **MATTHEW 7:24-27,** NIV

Q6. What do both of the homes in this story have in common?

Q7. What is different about the two builders?

Q8. What "big idea" was Jesus trying to get across in this message?

There are five classical methods for getting a personal and practical grasp on the Bible. Each has a different dynamic and benefit, but they are equally important. These five methods are

- Hearing: Listening to others as they share what they've learned from the Bible
- Reading: Reading the Bible to get an overview of its contents
- Studying: Focusing on small sections or ideas to gain in-depth understanding
- Memorizing: Committing short passages or verses to memory
- Meditating: Reflecting on the meaning of a verse, passage, or biblical idea over a period of time

As you continue your walk with Christ, learn to use each of these methods. Memorizing verses may sound difficult, but it can be a life-changing method for getting a grasp on the Bible. We suggest you begin by memorizing the key verses at the beginning of each lesson in this study.

Q9. What verse from this study will you memorize this week?

SUMMARY

The Bible is essential for our spiritual journey. It is more than a collection of stories or words of wisdom. It is God's letter to His people. It is absolutely true and reliable. It was supernaturally given and preserved. It will remain when man's wisdom has faded into history. Understanding, believing, and applying it to our lives is the only sure way to gain true meaning and success in this life.

PRAYER

Father, thank You that Your Word reveals who You are and guides my path. Teach me to trust in what You say, and forgive me when I stray from it to go my own direction. Use Your Word to change my thinking, realign my values, and alter my behavior so that my life will honor You. Help me live today in light of Your eternal truth.

LESSON 15

PRAYER

Prayer is the breath of the soul. It allows God access to our lives and needs.
Prayer is an attitude of the heart that humbly admits the need for help and seeks
the sunshine of God's grace. It is our personal communication with the living God.

*This is what I want you to do: Ask the Father for whatever is in
keeping with the things I've revealed to you. Ask in my name,
according to my will, and he'll most certainly give it to you.
Your joy will be a river overflowing its banks!*

JOHN 16:23-24

GEORGE MÜLLER WAS the founder of the Ashley Down Orphanage in
Bristol, England, during the late 1800s. With no resources except prayer
and faith in God, Mr. Müller saw God provide daily for the needs of
his children.

One day as Mr. Müller was traveling on a steamer to Quebec, the
ship encountered a dense fog off the coast of Newfoundland. Mr. Müller
approached the captain and said, "Captain, I have come to tell you that
I must be in Quebec on Saturday afternoon."

"It is impossible," the captain replied. "Do you know how dense
this fog is?"

"No," Müller replied, "my eye is not on the density of the fog, but on
the living God, who controls every circumstance of my life."

Mr. Müller prayed a simple prayer that would have been fitting in
any child's Sunday school class. His prayer went something like this:

"O Lord, if it is consistent with Thy will, please remove this fog in five minutes. You know the engagement You made for me in Quebec for Saturday. I believe it is Your will."

The captain was also going to pray, but Müller stopped him and said, "First, you do not believe God will do it; and second, I believe He has done it. And there is no need whatever for you to pray about it."

When they walked out of the chart room, the fog was gone. By Saturday afternoon, Mr. Müller was in Quebec.[1]

Prayer is a major resource for our walk with Christ. It is our moment-by-moment communication link with God. It is simple enough for a child to use yet so complex that great theologians don't fully understand it. It is practical yet a mystery.

Jesus expects us to pray. In this lesson we will look at some basic principles of prayer that will help you as you begin your walk with Christ.

Q1. **Which of the following statements have been true of your thinking?**

_____ I pray only when I run out of my own resources and need help.

_____ Prayer is for the religious part of my life.

_____ Prayer requires a special vocabulary.

_____ Prayer is a state of mind.

_____ Prayer requires some merit on my part to be effective.

_____ Prayer is like talking to myself.

In the Bible, prayer can refer to

- Worship—Reflecting on who God is through praise
- Thanksgiving—Reviewing what God has done and expressing gratitude
- Confession—Admitting our failures and shortcomings
- Petition—Requesting help from God

Prayer is our part of a relational dialogue with God. Through the Scriptures, God speaks to us; through prayer, we speak to Him. Prayer can be formal or informal, private or public. It can be done in a church or in our homes. It can be done for hours or in a matter of seconds. It can be spoken or thought.

PRAYER AND ACCESS

The writer of Hebrews said in Hebrews 4:14-16,

> Now that we know what we have—Jesus, this great High Priest with ready access to God—let's not let it slip through our fingers. We don't have a priest who is out of touch with our reality. He's been through weakness and testing, experienced it all—all but the sin. So let's walk right up to him and get what he is so ready to give. Take the mercy, accept the help.

The high priest was the top religious leader in the Old Testament form of worship. He was the only person who could go into the inner-most part of the Old Testament Tabernacle (the place of worship)—into the very presence of God. He was allowed to do this only once a year after elaborate preparations and sacrifices.

Q2. How is Jesus described in the previous passage?

Jesus, as our High Priest, dealt with sin once and for all with His sacrifice on the cross. He gained access for us into the presence of God. Because of Jesus' action, we are encouraged to boldly enter into God's presence through prayer. Jesus earned this privilege for us, and it is one of the rights of being a child of God.

PRAYER AND PETITIONS

Prayer is a response to the knock of Christ at the door of our hearts (see Revelation 3:20). As we realize our need for Him and His desire to help, prayer becomes an invitation for His involvement. Prayer requires humility and faith. Humility says, "I have a need," and faith says, "I believe God can help."

Jesus gave the following teaching on prayer in Matthew 6:5-13. This passage is often called the Lord's Prayer, though it might more accurately be called "our" prayer because it shows us how we ought to pray.

When you come before God, don't turn that into a theatrical production either. All these people making a regular show out of their prayers, hoping for stardom! Do you think God sits in a box seat?

Here's what I want you to do: Find a quiet, secluded place so you won't be tempted to role-play before God. Just be there as simply and honestly as you can manage. The focus will shift from you to God, and you will begin to sense his grace.

The world is full of so-called prayer warriors who are prayer-ignorant. They're full of formulas and programs and advice, peddling techniques for getting what you want from God. Don't fall for that nonsense. This is your Father you are dealing with, and he knows better than you what you need. With a God like this loving you, you can pray very simply. Like this:

Our Father in heaven,
Reveal who you are.
Set the world right;
Do what's best—
    as above, so below.
Keep us alive with three square meals.
Keep us forgiven with you and forgiving others.

Keep us safe from ourselves and the Devil.

You're in charge!

You can do anything you want!

You're ablaze in beauty!

    Yes. Yes. Yes.

Imagine how surprised the disciples must have been when Jesus gave them a model for prayer that was so simple and short. It was likely in sharp contrast to the long-winded prayers they might have previously thought were proper. Yet in this brief prayer, we are taught the essentials of effective communication with God.

Q3. **What does this passage tell us are the important components of prayer?**

Q4. **What instructions did Jesus give regarding prayer?**

Did you notice that this prayer begins with a focus on God, moves to a focus on others, and ends with a focus on self? Effective prayer is not simply designed to meet our personal needs—giving God a "to-do list." It encompasses so much more than that.

PRAYER AND GOD'S NATURE

Jesus told several parables (stories crafted to communicate specific lessons) to help people understand the value of prayer. One is found in Luke 11:5-9:

> He said, "Imagine what would happen if you went to a friend in the middle of the night and said, 'Friend, lend me three loaves of bread. An old friend traveling through just showed up, and I don't have a thing on hand.'

"The friend answers from his bed, 'Don't bother me. The door's locked; my children are all down for the night; I can't get up to give you anything.'

"But let me tell you, even if he won't get up because he's a friend, if you stand your ground, knocking and waking all the neighbors, he'll finally get up and get you whatever you need.

"Here's what I'm saying:

Ask and you'll get;

Seek and you'll find;

Knock and the door will open."

God can be compared with the friend in the parable. Though God may at times appear to be reluctant to answer our prayers, He is actually causing us to ask, seek, and knock with our whole hearts. Could it be that our Father is inviting us to "bother" Him with our requests?

Q5. **Knowing that God is eager to respond, is generous, and doesn't forget, why do you think He tells us to ask persistently or continually?**

While we don't know the mystery behind prayer, there are many good reasons to pray. Praying strengthens our faith. As we continually come before God with our worship and needs, we learn to trust and rely on Him. We develop a new perspective and mind-set. We move from independence to dependence.

As we persist in prayer, we also learn to listen to God. God is not like a heavenly Santa Claus giving us what we want at the moment we want it, but rather He works in our hearts to teach us to desire what is good and right. In prayer, God aligns the desires of our hearts to fit with His perfect plan. Consistent prayer also unleashes God's power. God has committed Himself to respond to the prayers of His people. Prayer is how we partner with God in doing what He wants done.

God answers prayer in one of three ways: "yes," "no," and "not yet." It's in the "not yet" that persistent prayer becomes most valuable. When we faithfully bring our needs to Him in prayer, He is not offended. In fact, He delights in our continued dependence.

Sometimes I pray as though God were a reluctant benefactor who needs to be convinced that what I'm asking for is worthwhile. In Luke 11:10-13, Jesus reminds us how we should think about God when we pray:

> Don't bargain with God. Be direct. Ask for what you need. This is not a cat-and-mouse, hide-and-seek game we're in. If your little boy asks for a serving of fish, do you scare him with a live snake on his plate? If your little girl asks for an egg, do you trick her with a spider? As bad as you are, you wouldn't think of such a thing—you're at least decent to your own children. And don't you think the Father who conceived you in love will give the Holy Spirit when you ask him?

Q6. What does this passage tell us about God's nature?

Q7. What keeps you from being bold and confident when praying?

Sometimes we become discouraged in prayer because we don't hear the answer we expect or want from God. But prayer is not a blank check written to pull from God's resources. And God is not a vending machine, dispensing His power at the push of a button. He is a wise God who knows *what* is best and *when* it is best.

God responds to our prayers for our ultimate benefit and for His glory. God uses prayer to accomplish two major goals: our joy and His will. The apostle John wrote in 1 John 5:14-15: "How bold and free we then become in his presence, freely asking according to his will, sure that he's listening. And if we're confident that he's listening, we know that what we've asked for is as good as ours."

Q8. What does this passage teach us about prayer?

One of the best ways to keep prayer simple, consistent, and bold is to maintain a prayer list. A small, thin notebook or even a sheet of paper can serve as a handy system for jotting down prayers as well as a convenient way to record God's answers. Carry this notebook or paper with you so you can use it often.

SUMMARY

Prayer is more than a 911 call when we have an emergency. It is a privileged connection with the God of the universe. Prayer is a means to offer praise, give thanks, make requests, confess sins, and simply pour out our hearts to God. Our confidence in His willingness to hear and respond will give us the courage to keep our communication lines open with Him.

PRAYER

Thank You, Father, for the privilege of prayer. Thank You for being in touch with my every need. You know my deepest pain and my greatest joy. I know I can be honest with You because You know and accept me just as I am. Help me bring each care and need to You for Your divine touch. Keep my habit of self-centeredness and independence from driving a wedge in our relationship. Help me make prayer as natural to my spiritual journey as breathing is to my physical one.

THE HOLY SPIRIT

God's Spirit lives within each person who has received Christ by faith. Working with our spirits, the Holy Spirit teaches and comforts us as we journey through life with Christ. His presence brings us the ability to change our behavior and provides the power to live as we should.

I will talk to the Father, and he'll provide you another Friend so that you will always have someone with you.

JOHN 14:16

ON A FAMILY VACATION IN COLORADO, we signed up for a white-water rafting trip on the Arkansas River. We skipped over the first two difficulty levels and went straight for the "hang on for your lives" option.

We met our guide and then donned our iridescent wet suits, life preservers, and helmets. As we launched into the tranquil waters of the Arkansas River, our guide began a brief but important lecture and demonstration. His briefing included a litany of his qualifications: fifteen years' experience in rafting, leadership experience on every possible river in Colorado including the most difficult, six years' experience on this very river, and not a single passenger lost.

He then led our group in practicing the paddle maneuvers that would be critical once we reached the white water. We were instructed to respond to his commands instantly and vigorously. He explained that at times he would give different commands to each side of the raft that must be executed simultaneously. Finally, we were told what to do if someone fell overboard.

Then the white-water adventure began in earnest. There were times when, looking ahead, I (Ron) could see no way through the churning water and massive boulders that seemed to block our path. But each time, our guide strategically maneuvered us over, around, and through the obstacles. From his position at the stern of the raft, he calmly directed this novice crew safely through our scenic adventure.

God's Spirit is our expert guide through the "river" of life. He knows it well and promises to guide us safely over the rocks, around the boulders, and through the rough waters. He asks only that we listen, trust, and obey.

THE SPIRIT AND HIS NATURE

God's Spirit, also called the Holy Spirit or the Spirit of Christ, is the third person of the Trinity. While we can picture a father or a son, we don't have a complete picture of what a spirit looks like. This can lead people to see God's Spirit as simply a force rather than a person.

Yet the Bible relates all the personal attributes of God the Father and God the Son to the Spirit as well. The Spirit has a mind, emotions, and a will just like the Father and the Son. One of the definitions found in the dictionary for the word *person* is "a self-conscious or rational being."[1] The Bible does not describe the Holy Spirit as a mystical power or impersonal force. Rather He is a rational being—fully God and with a specific role in the lives of people.

Jesus taught His first followers about the Holy Spirit in John 16:12-15:

> I still have many things to tell you, but you can't handle them now.
> But when the Friend comes, the Spirit of the Truth, he will take

you by the hand and guide you into all the truth there is. He won't draw attention to himself, but will make sense out of what is about to happen and, indeed, out of all that I have done and said. He will honor me; he will take from me and deliver it to you. Everything the Father has is also mine. That is why I've said, "He takes from me and delivers to you."

Q1. How is the Spirit of God described in this passage?

Q2. Read the passage again and note the various things the Holy Spirit does.

The Spirit of God is sometimes referred to as the Servant of the Trinity. In this role, He brings attention to God the Son and God the Father rather than bringing attention to Himself. His servant role does not in any way diminish the importance of His work or the need to understand His role in our lives, as we will see later in the study.

One of the promises that Christ made to those who put their faith in Him was that His Spirit would actually take up residence in their lives. Every believer is indwelt by God's Spirit, as explained in 1 Corinthians: "Don't you know that you yourselves are God's temple and that God's Spirit dwells in your midst?" (3:16, NIV).

The Bible also says that we are baptized by the Spirit. The term *baptize* means "to place into." This term was used to describe the tempering of metal by placing it into water or the coloring of cloth by dipping it into a dye. Likewise, we are "placed into" the body of Christ by God's Spirit. In 1 Corinthians we read, "We were all baptized by one Spirit so as to form one body—whether Jews or Gentiles, slave or free—and we were all given the one Spirit to drink" (12:13, NIV).

Learning to live in the reality of the indwelling Spirit of God is key to walking with Christ. His presence in us is more than a nice religious idea; it is absolutely critical to our relationship with God.

Q3. What practical difference does it make that God's Spirit lives in you?

Jesus promised that He would never leave His disciples. While physically present, He was limited by time and space. And so He left this world—in an event we call the Ascension—to send the Holy Spirit to dwell in all believers.

THE SPIRIT AND HIS WORK

Our daughter was in her first musical production during her junior year of college. In preparation for her role, she read the script to understand the story and get to know her character. However, reading the script was just one aspect of the preparation needed for her performance. She also needed a director who could coach her on how to act, talk, and sing. The director was key to developing and blending the talents of each person into a performance that would honor the intent of the playwright and composer.

The Lord has given each of us a role to play in this life. It is a role filled with meaning and purpose. We learn our part as we study the Bible (the script). But we also need the Holy Spirit, who explains what we are to do and empowers us to do it. We can't honor the intent of our creator without the power of the Spirit working in and through our lives.

As a new Christian, you may have some concerns regarding your ability to live the Christian life.

Q4. **Put a mark next to any of the following statements that describe you:**

_____ I don't know if I'll ever understand the Bible.

_____ Sometimes I don't know the right questions to ask.

_____ My life is a tangled mess, and I can't change my old habits.

_____ I try to live the right way, but I get tripped up and fail.

_____ I'm afraid that God's standards are too high and I won't be able to meet them.

_____ Other:

Our role, Jesus summarized, is to love God with all our hearts and to love our neighbors as ourselves. This is simple to say but impossible to do on our own. To accomplish this purpose, we need the constant coaching and empowering of God's Spirit. Jesus explained the role of God's Spirit in John 14:25-27:

> I'm telling you these things while I'm still living with you. The Friend, the Holy Spirit whom the Father will send at my request, will make everything plain to you. He will remind you of all the things I have told you. I'm leaving you well and whole. That's my parting gift to you. Peace. I don't leave you the way you're used to being left—feeling abandoned, bereft. So don't be upset. Don't be distraught.

Q5. **What did Jesus say the Spirit will do for you?**

Q6. **What do these verses say will be the result of God's Spirit at work within us?**

Other people will come alongside you with a word of encouragement and direction as you live the life Jesus gave you. God designed the church (His followers) to be a resource on your journey. However, people aren't always there to help—and sometimes they simply let you down. God's Spirit is always present, always adequate, and always willing to guide and direct your life.

THE SPIRIT AND HIS IMPACT

God's Spirit not only leads and directs us; He also brings about real change.

Q7. **As you read Romans 8:9-17 below, circle the things that change or are different when God's Spirit is in you.**

If God himself has taken up residence in your life, you can hardly be thinking more of yourself than of him. Anyone, of course, who has not welcomed this invisible but clearly present God, the Spirit of Christ, won't know what we're talking about. But for you who welcome him, in whom he dwells—even though you still experience all the limitations of sin—you yourself experience life on God's terms. It stands to reason, doesn't it, that if the alive-and-present God who raised Jesus from the dead moves into your life, he'll do the same thing in you that he did in Jesus, bringing you alive to himself? When God lives and breathes in you (and he does, as surely as he did in Jesus), you are delivered from that dead life. With his Spirit living in you, your body will be as alive as Christ's!

So don't you see that we don't owe this old do-it-yourself life one red cent. There's nothing in it for us, nothing at all. The best thing to do is give it a decent burial and get on with your new life. God's Spirit beckons. There are things to do and places to go!

142

This resurrection life you received from God is not a timid, grave-tending life. It's adventurously expectant, greeting God with a childlike "What's next, Papa?" God's Spirit touches our spirits and confirms who we really are. We know who he is, and we know who we are: Father and children. And we know we are going to get what's coming to us—an unbelievable inheritance! We go through exactly what Christ goes through. If we go through the hard times with him, then we're certainly going to go through the good times with him!

Wherever the Spirit of God is, there is power. Jesus explained it to His early disciples like this: "You will receive power when the Holy Spirit has come upon you; and you shall be My witnesses both in Jerusalem, and in all Judea and Samaria, and even to the remotest part of the earth" (Acts 1:8, NASB).

God's Spirit brings power to live life as God designed it. His Spirit brings inside-out change. He actually changes us to reflect His character and nature. Over time we will bear the family likeness more and more, as described in 2 Corinthians 3:18: "We all, who with unveiled faces contemplate the Lord's glory, are being transformed into his image with ever-increasing glory, which comes from the Lord, who is the Spirit" (NIV).

The apostle Paul described this change to reflect God's likeness as bearing the "fruit of the Spirit." Paul gave a list of these character qualities in Galatians 5:22-23: "The fruit of the Spirit is love, joy, peace, forbearance, kindness, goodness, faithfulness, gentleness and self-control. Against such things there is no law" (NIV).

The term *fruit* provides a word picture of the character change in a Christian as a result of the work of the Spirit. To understand this word picture, we can reflect on the nature of fruit as we know it in the natural world. Consider these "fruit facts":

1. Each tree naturally bears only one type of fruit.
2. The amount of fruit a tree is able to produce depends on (a) the maturity of the tree, (b) the amount of nutrients available and absorbed, and (c) the presence or absence of disease.
3. A deep root system gives a fruit tree greater access to water and stability.

These facts of nature give us insight into how we can cooperate with God's Spirit so that His fruit (a spiritual nature) is produced in our lives.

Christians should expect to produce the fruit of the Spirit because they have the reality of the Spirit within them. Loving our enemies, the unlovable, or the ungrateful, for example, is an unselfish kind of love that comes only from the nature of God. In order to produce spiritual fruit, we need to

1. Grow in maturity
2. Take in the nourishment of God's Word
3. Deal with the presence of sin that robs us of spiritual health

Spiritual fruit will grow when we develop deep spiritual roots in Christ and His Word. These roots will provide strength and stability in difficult times.

For the Spirit of God to change us, we need to not only acknowledge His presence in our lives, but also actively cooperate with Him by following His directions and relying on His supernatural power. We will do well to follow the advice given in Proverbs 3:5-6:

> Trust GOD from the bottom of your heart;
>> don't try to figure out everything on your own.
> Listen for GOD's voice in everything you do, everywhere you go;
>> he's the one who will keep you on track.

Q8. **What are specific ways you can cooperate with the Spirit of God?**

Be like a tree - based on the Fruits of the spirit. Pg 144 1st par

Q9. **How has God changed your life since you put your faith in Him?**

Calmer, patient, not as anxi

Q10. **What are some things you would like to see change in the future as you continue your journey with Christ?**

speak/have more time with him

SUMMARY

God lives in us through His Spirit. His presence means that we are never alone. God's Spirit is always available to guide, direct, and comfort us along the journey. As we respond to His presence, we are changed into His likeness. That likeness will increasingly reflect the true nature and character of God.

PRAYER

Father, thank You for the way Your Spirit works in my life. Thank You that He gives me an understanding of who You are and helps me live a life that honors You. On my own I would fail, but You have filled me with Your presence so I am never alone. Help me listen to Your Spirit and treat people today with love and kindness.

LESSON 17
GRACE

Grace is an amazing truth that God accepts us, not because of what we have done, but because of what Christ did for us. Grace is the foundation for our security with God, the source of forgiveness, and the power to live as we should. Grace is the atmosphere that enables us to experience freedom in our relationship with Jesus.

[God] has saved us and called us to a holy life—not because of anything we have done but because of his own purpose and grace. This grace was given us in Christ Jesus before the beginning of time.
2 TIMOTHY 1:9, NIV

KING DAVID IS ONE of the most famous Old Testament characters in the Bible. The second king of Israel, he was called a man after God's own heart. As a young man, he delivered Israel from oppression when he killed a giant warrior called Goliath with his slingshot. He was anointed by God to be king of Israel and then spent the next ten years as a fugitive, running from the current king, King Saul. David finally became king at the age of thirty after years of self-exile in caves and the desert.

After King David set up his administration, he did an amazing, countercultural act. He asked his advisers, "Is there no one still alive from the house of Saul to whom I can show God's kindness?" (2 Samuel 9:3, NIV). Rather than eliminate any possible competition from the previous king—a king who had threatened to kill him—David wanted to honor Saul's descendants. He found just one relative: a grandson of King Saul named Mephibosheth, who had become permanently injured while escaping the aftermath of King Saul's demise. For years he had been hiding, fearing reprisal from a new king and his party.

King David demonstrated grace rather than retribution in dealing with this grandson of King Saul. He restored Mephibosheth's family wealth, provided managers for his land, and invited him into the royal family circle as a permanent honored guest (see 2 Samuel 9).

King David reflected the grace of God in his attitude and actions to this surprised young man. All Mephibosheth had to do was accept it!

GRACE AND ACCEPTANCE

In most settings, the basis of acceptance is performance. Business, education, and sports all operate based on performance. Either you do your job well or you're let go; you win or you don't play. Value is primarily determined by how well you do what you are called to do. Merit, in its various forms, is the fuel that drives the engine of success and acceptance.

The Bible introduces a radically different definition of value: the concept of grace, or unmerited favor. The phrase *kindness of God* is used in the Old Testament to communicate God's grace. Showing grace means to give favor to someone who doesn't deserve it and would never be able to earn it.

Q1. Describe a situation or environment you've been in that was based on grace instead of merit. How did it make you feel?

We thrive on merit. We like to assert our abilities and experience pride in what we do. Why? Because we can take credit for the results. Merit keeps us in the driver's seat. We are in control. Merit and performance are key to world religions, too—every religion *except* Christianity.

But even in Christianity, people often get it wrong—they try to get to heaven based on their good behavior. When asked, "Why should God let you into heaven?" many people respond, "Because the good that I have done is greater than the bad!" In other words, they believe they have earned it. As Bill Hybels, pastor of Willow Creek Community Church, often puts it, the message of Christ is "done," not "do." Christ did it all, and there is nothing left for us to do.

To better understand grace, it's important to understand God's holiness and love. God's holiness means that He can't tolerate sin. His love means that He is deeply compassionate and forgiving. God's holiness and love are like the two parts of a cross: His holiness is the vertical piece, and His love the horizontal. Where the two meet is grace, the divine connection between absolute holiness and unconditional love.

Suppose a UPS driver comes to your door and hands you a package worth more than you could ever earn in a lifetime. He tells you that it is addressed to you from an anonymous benefactor and that there are no strings attached. All you have to do is sign the form saying you received it. You could refuse the package, unwilling to accept it unless you could do something to earn it. Or you could sign your name on the form, fully believing you did earn it. Both actions would be unexpected and unlikely. Perhaps instead, even though you knew you didn't deserve it, you would accept the gift.

God's gift of life is worth more than you could ever earn in many lifetimes. He offers it to you with no strings attached and simply waits for you to accept it. Paul summed it up like this in Ephesians 2:8-9: "Saving is all his idea, and all his work. All we do is trust him enough to let him do it. It's God's gift [grace] from start to finish! We don't play the major role. If we did, we'd probably go around bragging that we'd done the whole thing!"

Q2. When it comes to grace, what is God's role and what is our role?

It's not unusual for people who begin their walk with Christ by accepting God's unmerited favor to soon feel they must perform in order to keep His favor.

Q3. What does the previous passage from Ephesians say about continuing your walk with Christ by grace?

It's easy for merit thinking to creep into our relationship with Christ. When we are performing well (praying often, reading the Bible regularly, serving others selflessly), we may feel as if we have a greater audience with God. Yet God's grace means that we are at *no time* more acceptable to Him than when we first came to faith. We can't earn a better standing in the environment of grace.

In God's family, grace is a relational environment in which we are initially and permanently accepted. Grace, however, doesn't eliminate work, service, and obedience. In God's environment of grace we don't work or obey to *earn* God's favor, but we obey *because of* God's favor. The difference is significant. In the former, we are driven by performance, self-promotion, or fear. In the latter, we are motivated by thankfulness and gratitude.

GRACE AND FORGIVENESS

On our journey with Christ we will still face detours, wrong turns, and dead ends. What happens when we lose our way, take the wrong road, or wind up in a moral cul-de-sac?

Q4. Describe a time when you got lost. How did you feel? What did you do?

In our walk with Christ, sin is a hindrance. It is a big deal to God even if it is not in our culture. When we come to faith in Christ, God forgives our sin—past, present, and future. Sin is no longer held against us; our record is wiped clean by the blood of Christ. But although sin no longer affects our *acceptance* with God, it does affect our *relationship* with Him. Read what the apostle John wrote about sin in 1 John 1:5-10:

> This, in essence, is the message we heard from Christ and are passing on to you: God is light, pure light; there's not a trace of darkness in him.
>
> If we claim that we experience a shared life with him and continue to stumble around in the dark, we're obviously lying through our teeth—we're not *living* what we claim. But if we walk in the light, God himself being the light, we also experience a shared life with one another, as the sacrificed blood of Jesus, God's Son, purges all our sin.
>
> If we claim that we're free of sin, we're only fooling ourselves. A claim like that is errant nonsense. On the other hand, if we admit our sins—make a clean breast of them—he won't let us down; he'll be true to himself. He'll forgive our sins and purge us of all wrongdoing. If we claim that we've never sinned, we out-and-out contradict God—make a liar out of him. A claim like that only shows off our ignorance of God.

Q5. What does this passage say we should do about our sin?

Q6. What does God say He will do?

Q7. **Read the following passage. According to these verses, what are the primary sources of sin?**

> Don't love the world's ways. Don't love the world's goods. Love of the world squeezes out love for the Father. Practically everything that goes on in the world—wanting your own way, wanting everything for yourself, wanting to appear important—has nothing to do with the Father. It just isolates you from him.
>
> 1 JOHN 2:15-16

Luke recorded an interesting event in the life of Christ in Luke 7:36-50:

> One of the Pharisees asked him over for a meal. He went to the Pharisee's house and sat down at the dinner table. Just then a woman of the village, the town harlot, having learned that Jesus was a guest in the home of the Pharisee, came with a bottle of very expensive perfume and stood at his feet, weeping, raining tears on his feet. Letting down her hair, she dried his feet, kissed them, and anointed them with the perfume. When the Pharisee who had invited him saw this, he said to himself, "If this man was the prophet I thought he was, he would have known what kind of woman this is who is falling all over him."
>
> Jesus said to him, "Simon, I have something to tell you."
>
> "Oh? Tell me."
>
> "Two men were in debt to a banker. One owed five hundred silver pieces, the other fifty. Neither of them could pay up, and so the banker canceled both debts. Which of the two would be more grateful?"
>
> Simon answered, "I suppose the one who was forgiven the most."

"That's right," said Jesus. Then turning to the woman, but speaking to Simon, he said, "Do you see this woman? I came to your home; you provided no water for my feet, but she rained tears on my feet and dried them with her hair. You gave me no greeting, but from the time I arrived she hasn't quit kissing my feet. You provided nothing for freshening up, but she has soothed my feet with perfume. Impressive, isn't it? She was forgiven many, many sins, and so she is very, very grateful. If the forgiveness is minimal, the gratitude is minimal."

Then he spoke to her: "I forgive your sins."

That set the dinner guests talking behind his back: "Who does he think he is, forgiving sins!"

He ignored them and said to the woman, "Your faith has saved you. Go in peace."

Q8. What do you learn about forgiveness from this passage?

Q9. How does this story demonstrate grace?

GRACE AND POWER

The term *grace* in the Bible also implies power. It is God's grace that frees us from being ruled by sin and begins to change us from the inside out. It is the grace of God that enables us to live as we should. Paul said in 2 Corinthians 12:9, "He [God] said to me, 'My grace is sufficient for you, for my power is made perfect in weakness.' Therefore I will boast all the more gladly about my weaknesses, so that Christ's power may rest on me" (NIV).

God not only empowers us to do what He wants but also gives us the desire to do it. God's grace in our lives changes our values and motives. The journey with Christ is not a matter of self-effort focused in a spiritual direction but of God's effort leading, guiding, and energizing every aspect of our lives.

Paul made an exciting discovery along his journey with Christ, but that discovery first appeared to him to be an inconvenient and unnecessary burden. Read what he discovered in 2 Corinthians 12:7-10 (emphasis added):

> Because of the extravagance of those revelations, and so I wouldn't get a big head, I was given the gift of a handicap to keep me in constant touch with my limitations. Satan's angel[1] did his best to get me down; what he in fact did was push me to my knees. No danger then of walking around high and mighty! At first I didn't think of it as a gift, and begged God to remove it. Three times I did that, and then he told me,
>
> *My grace is enough; it's all you need.*
> *My strength comes into its own in your weakness.*
>
> Once I heard that, I was glad to let it happen. I quit focusing on the handicap and began appreciating the gift. It was a case of Christ's strength moving in on my weakness. Now I take limitations in stride, and with good cheer, these limitations that cut me down to size—abuse, accidents, opposition, bad breaks. I just let Christ take over! And so the weaker I get, the stronger I become.

Q10.   What did Paul discover about God's grace?

Q11. What change in perspective occurred when Paul understood the significance of grace?

Q12. Describe a time in your life when you felt as Paul did upon receiving his "gift of a handicap." How could (or did) grace help you deal with your situation?

SUMMARY

Grace is real, but we can't earn what God freely gives. We can only accept it. Our walk with God is powered by His unmerited favor. It surrounds, supports, and enables us to walk with Him in freedom. Instead of basing our relationship with God on our work or performance, we can accept the gift of salvation given to us through Christ's death on the cross and enjoy His environment of grace.

PRAYER

Thank You, Father, for accepting me in Christ. Thank You that my journey with You starts and ends with Your grace. Supported by Your unmerited favor, I never need to fear rejection. I am always secure with You. Help me live today with an attitude of thankfulness for what You have done.

COMMUNITY

God has designed His followers to live and travel with companions in community. Christ leads this community (the church) and bonds it together through love. Each person has a significant and unique part to play within the whole community. Learning from and supporting one another is crucial for a successful journey.

Two can accomplish more than twice as much as one, for the results can be much better. If one falls, the other pulls him up; but if a man falls when he is alone, he's in trouble. Also, on a cold night, two under the same blanket gain warmth from each other, but how can one be warm alone? And one standing alone can be attacked and defeated, but two can stand back-to-back and conquer; three is even better, for a triple-braided cord is not easily broken.

ECCLESIASTES 4:9-12, TLB

ARON RALSTON IS an avid outdoorsman in excellent physical condition and a veteran climber of all fifty-nine of Colorado's "fourteeners" (mountains with peaks of at least 14,000 feet). In April 2003, Aron went on a one-day climb in a remote area of southeastern Utah . . . alone.

Forty miles from the nearest paved road and sixty feet up on a sheer rock face, Aron's right arm became pinned beneath a thousand-pound shifting boulder. Five days after becoming trapped and forty hours after he'd run out of water, he made a critical decision. His only hope for survival was to cut off his own arm. Using a pocketknife, he amputated his arm just below the elbow, applied a tourniquet, and then rappelled sixty-five feet to the canyon floor. After walking for several hours, he met other hikers, who helped bring in lifesaving medical assistance.

Our journey with Christ is too difficult and too dangerous to go solo. God never intended us to travel alone but rather with companions—in community—with each member supporting and contributing to the journey.

COMMUNITY AND COMPANIONSHIP

As Jesus prepared His followers for the future, He taught them to seek one quality—a quality that would become the hallmark of His touch on their lives. He said in John 13:34-35, "Let me give you a new command: Love one another. In the same way I loved you, you love one another. This is how everyone will recognize that you are my disciples—when they see the love you have for each other."

Some years later, Paul commended new believers in Thessalonica for this very quality: "You need to know, friends, that thanking God over and over for you is not only a pleasure; it's a must. We *have* to do it. Your faith is growing phenomenally; your love for each other is developing wonderfully. Why, it's only right that we give thanks" (2 Thessalonians 1:3).

Paul also gave a description of the kind of love that Jesus was talking about in 1 Corinthians 13:1-7.

Q1. **As you read this classic description of love, circle what love does and underline what love does not do.**

If I speak with human eloquence and angelic ecstasy but don't love, I'm nothing but the creaking of a rusty gate.

If I speak God's Word with power, revealing all his mysteries and making everything plain as day, and if I have faith that says to a mountain, "Jump," and it jumps, but I don't love, I'm nothing.

If I give everything I own to the poor and even go to the stake to be burned as a martyr, but I don't love, I've gotten nowhere. So, no matter what I say, what I believe, and what I do, I'm bankrupt without love.

Love never gives up.

Love cares more for others than for self.

Love doesn't want what it doesn't have.

Love doesn't strut,

Doesn't have a swelled head,

Doesn't force itself on others,

Isn't always "me first,"

Doesn't fly off the handle,

Doesn't keep score of the sins of others,

Doesn't revel when others grovel,

Takes pleasure in the flowering of truth,

Puts up with anything,

Trusts God always,

Always looks for the best,

Never looks back,

But keeps going to the end.

1 CORINTHIANS 13:1-7

Q2. How does this description of love compare with the way our culture defines love?

The Bible uses different words for love. One (*phileo*) refers to friendship—love that results because we admire someone or enjoy the company of that person. Another (*agape*) refers to a sacrificial love—love that is offered unconditionally. This has also been called divine love because it is the kind of love God has for us.

God wants this kind of agape love to permeate all our relationships. In the community of believers, it is a love that builds immediate closeness. You will be amazed at the kindred spirit you enjoy with other followers of Christ, even though you may not know them well. Outside the community of believers, it is a love that helps identify you as God's child.

COMMUNITY AND CONTRIBUTION

The book of Acts records the beginning of the church and, more specifically, how Christ followers began to experience community. In Acts 2, Peter presented the message of Christ to a large group of people. Thousands of them put their faith in Christ and became His followers. In doing so, they discovered a new and powerful support system. People who didn't know one another found a common bond and encouragement as they enjoyed community together.

Q3. **Read the following account from Acts 2:41-47 and describe the spiritual and physical support these new believers found in community.**

That day about three thousand took him at his word, were baptized and were signed up. They committed themselves to the teaching of the apostles, the life together, the common meal, and the prayers.

Everyone around was in awe—all those wonders and signs done through the apostles! And all the believers lived in a wonderful harmony, holding everything in common. They sold whatever they owned and pooled their resources so that each person's need was met.

They followed a daily discipline of worship in the Temple followed by meals at home, every meal a celebration, exuberant and joyful, as they praised God. People in general liked what they saw. Every day their number grew as God added those who were saved.

Q4. What were the results of this new community?

These early believers discovered that they could accomplish more together than they could alone. They also discovered that they needed one another. Throughout his letters, Paul reminded new believers that this community, the church (also called the "body of Christ" or the "body of believers"), is a unique and essential part of the faith journey.

Football provides us with a good analogy of how we work together in Christ's body. We are one team yet many players. Some positions may be more visible than others, yet all are equally important. A good coach assigns positions according to each player's physical design. Each player has a specific role that when carried out makes the team successful.

In a similar manner, every believer is essential to the team we call the church. As you walk with Christ, you will discover that you have special spiritual abilities. The Holy Spirit gave these gifts to you when you became a believer, and they will allow you to make a unique contribution to the community of believers.

COMMUNITY AND INFLUENCE

As we walk with Christ, there is a great deal to learn. We can learn much from fellow travelers—especially those who have been traveling a little longer than we have. Paul knew the importance of this kind of personal influence and how it helped with the development and training of new believers. Timothy was a young apprentice who often traveled with Paul. At the close of his life, Paul wrote a letter to Timothy in which he praised Timothy for learning from the influence of others during his spiritual journey. Here's an excerpt from that letter:

You know from watching me that I am not that kind of person. You know what I believe and the way I live and what I want. You know my faith in Christ and how I have suffered. You know my love for you, and my patience. You know how many troubles I have had as a result of my preaching the Good News. You know about all that was done to me while I was visiting in Antioch, Iconium, and Lystra, but the Lord delivered me. Yes, and those who decide to please Christ Jesus by living godly lives will suffer at the hands of those who hate him. In fact, evil men and false teachers will become worse and worse, deceiving many, they themselves having been deceived by Satan.

But you must keep on believing the things you have been taught. You know they are true, for you know that you can trust those of us who have taught you. You know how, when you were a small child, you were taught the holy Scriptures; and it is these that make you wise to accept God's salvation by trusting in Christ Jesus.

2 TIMOTHY 3:10-15, TLB

Q5.   What were some of the things Timothy learned from Paul?

Timothy also had others who influenced his life. Two are mentioned in 2 Timothy 1:5: "That precious memory triggers another: your honest faith—and what a rich faith it is, handed down from your grandmother Lois to your mother Eunice, and now to you!"

Q6.   Who have been significant influences in your Christian walk?

Q7. Who do you know who could be a "Paul," or a mentor, to you as you continue your spiritual journey?

Ask God to bring into your life someone whom you respect for his or her spiritual faith. Then be courageous and ask this person to consider being a mentor for you in your spiritual journey. The role of a mentor isn't simply to teach you; it is to teach you so that you can then teach others. Read what Paul revealed about the purpose of mentoring in 2 Timothy 2:2: "The things you have heard me say in the presence of many witnesses entrust to reliable people who will also be qualified to teach others" (NIV).

Timothy was not only personally mentored by Paul, but his apprenticeship occurred in the context of community. In that community, Timothy had three types of relationships: with a mentor, with his peers, and with those he taught. Paul told Timothy not only to be a learner but also to become a teacher. Timothy was to be a spiritual link in a chain of learners and fellow travelers.

As you continue to grow in your relationship with Christ and in your understanding and application of the Bible, look for someone you can influence—perhaps a friend who is interested in how you got started on your journey with Christ. At some point in your journey, you will meet someone who is what you are now: a new believer. Your walk with Christ can offer wisdom and encouragement to that believer. Hang on to this book. You may even want to use it to help guide this new believer.

May God be with you as you continue your walk of faith.

SUMMARY

God designed us to travel our spiritual journey in the companionship of others. This community of believers is uniquely bonded together by the power of love. Living in community, we are interdependent—we need one another to finish the journey successfully.

PRAYER

Thank You, Father, that I don't have to travel this journey alone. You have given me traveling companions to share with and learn from. Teach me to love my companions as You love me. Help me be a spiritual link in the chain of relationships that will build up Your community of faith.

SUMMARY

USE THE FOLLOWING CHART to review the lessons you have just completed. You may want to show someone else what you have been learning about your journey with Christ.

LESSON	KEY VERSE	SCRIPTURES	KEY CONCEPTS
Faith	Proverbs 3:5-6	Hebrews 11:1, 6; Luke 8:40-56	Faith and Reality; Faith and God; Faith and Action
The Word	Psalm 119:19-20	Psalm 19:7-11; 2 Timothy 3:16-17; Matthew 7:24-27	The Bible and Truth; The Bible and Success; The Bible and Obedience
Prayer	John 16:23-24	Hebrews 4:14-16; Matthew 6:5-13; Luke 11:5-13	Prayer and Access; Prayer and Petitions; Prayer and God's Nature
The Holy Spirit	John 14:16	John 14:25-27; 16:12-15; Romans 8:9-17	The Spirit and His Nature; The Spirit and His Work; The Spirit and His Impact
Grace	2 Timothy 1:9	Ephesians 2:8-9; Luke 7:36-50; 2 Corinthians 12:7-10	Grace and Acceptance; Grace and Forgiveness; Grace and Power
Community	Ecclesiastes 4:9-12	1 Corinthians 13:1-7	Community and Companionship; Community and Contribution; Community and Influence

APPENDIX 1
BEGINNING YOUR WALK

AS YOU CONSIDER your journey with Christ, it is important to understand how a relationship with Christ is established.

GOD'S PURPOSE

The Bible begins by showing us that God created man (men and women) to share

US ——————— GOD

His image and an intimate relationship with Him. Man and woman were in perfect union with God. However, that union was broken by their decision to become morally independent from God. That independence is also called disobedience or sin.

Sin resulted in alienation or separation from God. The intimacy was gone. People and God no longer experienced a personal relationship. People became spiritually dead. That condition has been passed down through every generation since Adam and Eve.

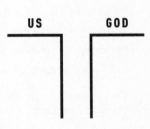

OUR PROBLEM

The Bible describes humanity's problem in a statement found in Romans 5:12:

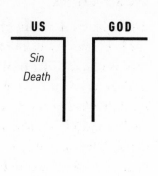

> You know the story of how Adam landed us in the dilemma we're in—first sin, then death, and no one exempt from either sin or death. That sin disturbed relations with God in everything and everyone.

Death can also be described as separation. Death in its various forms resulted from people's sin and is experienced in every area of life: physical, emotional, social, psychological, and spiritual. Ultimately, death leads to an eternal separation from God and His purpose.

GOD'S PLAN

The Bible also reveals God's plan. Read this statement from John 3:16:

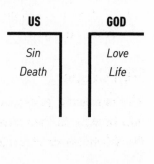

> This is how much God loved the world: He gave his Son, his one and only Son. And this is why: so that no one need be destroyed; by believing in him, anyone can have a whole and lasting life.

God desires to reestablish the intimacy that was lost and give us life that is eternal.

GOD'S PROVISION

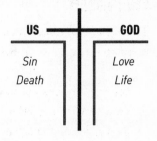

Throughout human history people have tried to reach God, primarily through good works. Yet our good works are always inadequate to span the gulf created by sin. Self-effort in any form falls short of God's standard for holiness. His holiness demands that our sin be accounted for, and His love demands a response of grace. God's answer to this dilemma was to put His love on the line for us by offering His Son in sacrificial death to pay the price for our sin.

Read Romans 5:8 to see how this provision works: "God demonstrates His own love toward us, in that while we were yet sinners, Christ died for us" (NASB). Notice the progression as it follows the verse: God—loves—us—sinners—Christ—died—for us.

Jesus was God's provision for the problem of our sin. His death and resurrection provided the bridge that can reunite us with God. It is the *only* means by which this union can be restored. Jesus said, "I am the way, and the truth, and the life; no one comes to the Father but through Me" (John 14:6, NASB).

OUR PRIVILEGE

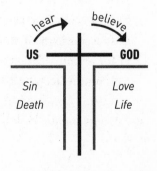

The statement in John 5:24 (NASB) explains how an individual can cross over the bridge that Christ has provided. Jesus said,

> Truly, truly, I say to you, he who hears My word, and believes Him who sent Me, has eternal life, and does not come into judgment, but has passed out of death into life.

From this statement, notice what Christ is offering us:

1. Eternal life
2. No judgment
3. Passage from death to life

Notice what is necessary to receive this offer:

1. Hear His word
2. Believe in Him (the Father) who sent Christ

The term *belief* means more than acknowledgment of facts or information. "Believe in" means to "trust in, commit to, rely upon, or receive." We become children of God and are reunited in a personal relationship with Him when we make a personal commitment of faith. God's provision has been extended to us. It is a gift. And as a gift, we cannot work for it; we can only receive it.

Have you personally put your faith in Jesus Christ as your way to God? If not, would you be willing by faith to accept Christ as your bridge to God right now? You can express this step of faith in a simple prayer in which you tell God:

1. I recognize that I am separate from You as a result of my sin.
2. I recognize that Christ was Your provision for me—that He died for my sin.
3. I want to accept by faith Your gift of forgiveness through Christ.
4. I thank You for Your forgiveness and for accepting me as part of Your family.

APPENDIX 2
WHO I AM IN CHRIST

Understanding your identity in Christ is absolutely essential
for your success at living a victorious Christian life.

D. NEIL ANDERSON

THIS STUDY REPRESENTS only a part of your walk with Christ. Voices from the past and present will constantly challenge what you learn. Discovering who you are in Christ can help you on your journey.

Read the following statements and verses aloud, taking time after each to allow the truth to capture your mind and heart. You may want to refer often to this list.

I AM . . . GOD'S WORKMANSHIP.

We are His workmanship, created in Christ Jesus for good works,
which God prepared beforehand so that we would walk in them.

EPHESIANS 2:10, NASB

I AM . . . THE SALT AND LIGHT OF THE EARTH.

You are the salt of the earth; but if the salt has become tasteless,
how can it be made salty again? It is no longer good for anything,
except to be thrown out and trampled under foot by men. You are
the light of the world. A city set on a hill cannot be hidden.

MATTHEW 5:13-14, NASB

I AM . . . A BRANCH OF THE VINE.

I am the vine, you are the branches; he who abides in Me and I in him, he bears much fruit, for apart from Me you can do nothing.

JOHN 15:5, NASB

I AM . . . GOD'S TEMPLE.

Do you not know that you are a temple of God and that the Spirit of God dwells in you?

1 CORINTHIANS 3:16, NASB

I AM . . . AN AMBASSADOR FOR CHRIST.

Therefore, we are ambassadors for Christ, as though God were making an appeal through us; we beg you on behalf of Christ, be reconciled to God. He made Him who knew no sin to be sin on our behalf, so that we might become the righteousness of God in Him.

2 CORINTHIANS 5:20-21, NASB

I AM . . . SEATED WITH CHRIST IN THE HEAVENLY REALMS.

God raised us up with Christ and seated us with him in the heavenly realms in Christ Jesus.

EPHESIANS 2:6, NIV

I AM . . . GOD'S CHILD.

As many as received Him, to them He gave the right to become children of God, even to those who believe in His name.

JOHN 1:12, NASB

I AM . . . CHRIST'S FRIEND.

No longer do I call you slaves, for the slave does not know what his master is doing; but I have called you friends, for all things that I have heard from My Father I have made known to you.

JOHN 15:15, NASB

I AM . . . BOUGHT WITH A PRICE AND BELONG TO CHRIST.

Do you not know that your body is a temple of the Holy Spirit who is in you, whom you have from God, and that you are not your own? For you have been bought with a price: therefore glorify God in your body.

1 CORINTHIANS 6:19-20, NASB

I AM . . . A MEMBER OF CHRIST'S BODY.

Now you are Christ's body, and individually members of it.

1 CORINTHIANS 12:27, NASB

I AM . . . COMPLETE IN CHRIST.

In Him you have been made complete, and He is the head over all rule and authority.

COLOSSIANS 2:10, NASB

I AM . . . A CITIZEN OF HEAVEN.

Our citizenship is in heaven, from which also we eagerly wait for a Savior, the Lord Jesus Christ.

PHILIPPIANS 3:20, NASB

I AM . . . BORN OF GOD.

For this reason therefore the Jews were seeking all the more to kill Him, because He not only was breaking the Sabbath, but also was calling God His own Father, making Himself equal with God.

JOHN 5:18, NASB

APPENDIX 3
NEXT STEPS IN YOUR WALK WITH CHRIST

THE BIBLE IS ONE of the most important assets we have for our journey with Christ. It is the revelation of who God is, told through the stories of men and women who encountered Him. The first part, called the Old Testament, starts with Creation and ends about five hundred years before the birth of Christ. It is the story line of God's interaction with a group of people called the Israelites.

The second part, called the New Testament, starts with the birth of Jesus. The first four books are called Gospels and tell about the life of Christ from four different perspectives. The remaining books (or letters) were written to various groups of new believers during the first century.

BIBLE READING

We want to encourage you to begin reading about the life of Christ. The Gospel of Luke is a great place to start. Luke gives a fairly comprehensive overview of what Jesus did and taught. If you don't have your own Bible, you can visit a Christian bookstore and purchase either a New Testament or a complete Bible. You may want to start with a translation that is easy to understand, such as the New Living Translation or *The Message*.

Begin by reading one story or chapter every day. As you read, be sure to underline, circle, or highlight things that stand out to you. You might even put a question mark next to parts you don't understand. You can refer to them later with a mentor or someone you trust.

When the apostle Paul, writer of most of the New Testament, first encountered Christ, he asked two questions that are still relevant today. The first was "Who are you?" and the second (implied in the text) was "What would you have me do?" (Acts 9:5-6). Reading Scripture with these two questions in mind is a good way to reflect on what you are reading. God wants to reveal Himself to you and lead you into His Kingdom kind of life. As you read the Bible and pray, you form a dialogue with God. He speaks to you through His Word, and you speak to Him in prayer.

SCRIPTURE MEMORY

Memorizing Scripture is a powerful way to begin transforming our minds to think like Jesus. We memorize things we want to recall quickly, such as our phone number, our address, and critical passwords. Memorizing special verses from the Bible allows us to quickly recall important concepts or promises God has given us.

We encourage you to begin memorizing some of the key verses found at the beginning of each lesson in *Beginning the Walk*—especially those verses in the third section, "Jesus the Life." Write them down on a 3 x 5 card or a blank business card so you can carry them with you and review them during the day. Memorize one phrase at a time until you can say the whole verse from memory. Try to review each verse you memorize every day in order to get it firmly fixed in your mind. For most people it takes a daily review for seven weeks to really get it memorized.

The process of fixing Scripture verses in your memory gives the Holy Spirit the fuel to change your life. Bible reading and Scripture memory are like electrical plugs that tap into God's power. That power is available, waiting for us to connect to it.

SUGGESTIONS FOR MEMORIZING BIBLE VERSES

1. Identify a verse that is meaningful to you.
2. Write it on a 3 x 5 card. Include the reference.
3. Read it frequently.
4. Memorize it one phrase at a time until you can remember the whole statement.
5. Practice saying the verse from memory. Quote the reference at the beginning and end.
6. Review the verse every day for seven weeks.
7. Share the verse—and what it means to you—with a friend.

NOTES

LESSON 1: NEW CONNECTION
1. See, for example, Deuteronomy 10:14-18; Joshua 24:19-20; Job 34:10-20.
2. M. G. Easton, *Illustrated Bible Dictionary*, 3rd ed. (London: Thomas Nelson, 1897), http://www.biblestudytools.com/dictionaries/eastons-bible-dictionary/trinity.html.

LESSON 2: NEW CREATION
1. "1976: Soviet Pilot Lands Russian MIG Fighter Plane in Japan," This Day in History, http://www.history.com/this-day-in-history/soviet-pilot-lands-russian-mig-fighter-plane-in-japan.
2. See, for example, Ephesians 1:1 (NASB).
3. W. E. Vine, *An Expository Dictionary of New Testament Words* (Westwood, NJ: Fleming H. Revell, 1940), 226. The New Living Translation also refers to people who are "called" (see 1 Corinthians 1:2).

LESSON 8: HIS SHEEP
1. See W. Phillip Keller, *The Shepherd Trilogy: A Shepherd Looks at the 23rd Psalm / A Shepherd Looks at the Good Shepherd / A Shepherd Looks at the Lamb of God* (Grand Rapids, MI: Zondervan, 1996).

LESSON 9: HIS CHILD
1. James Strong, *Strong's Exhaustive Concordance of the Bible* (Peabody, MA: Hendrickson, 2009).

LESSON 12: HIS DWELLING PLACE
1. Robert Boyd Munger, *My Heart—Christ's Home: A Story for Old and Young* (Downers Grove, IL: IVP, 1954), 5.

LESSON 15: PRAYER
1. Albert Sims, ed., *George Mueller: Man of Faith* (Chicago: Moody, n.d.), 29–31; reprint of Albert Sims, ed., *An Hour with George Mueller: The Man of Faith to Whom God Gave Millions* (Grand Rapids, MI: Zondervan, n.d.).

LESSON 16: THE HOLY SPIRIT
1. *The American College Dictionary*, s.v. "person."

LESSON 17: GRACE
1. Satan has many spirits that follow him. These are sometimes called "demons" or "fallen angels."

ABOUT THE AUTHORS

RON AND MARY BENNETT joined the staff of The Navigators in 1970. They have led ministries on college campuses, in the military, and in the community. Ron served on the national leadership team of the Navigator Church Ministries, where he also authored *Intentional Disciplemaking* and coauthored *The Adventure of Discipling Others*. Mary is the author of a Bible study called *Fire Resistant Parenting*, and together they led the team that developed the HighQuest discipleship series.

We want to express our appreciation to Bob Walz for his outstanding coaching and invaluable advice in the development of this material. His insight and encouragement were a constant source of energy and motivation.